It is my sincere desire that the owner of this book would find within the pages healing that only comes from our loving and caring Abba-daddy!

I speak a blessing over your life that you will come to know your Abba-daddy in the full measure of his abiding mercy and power that is available to his children.

Sincerely in His Service,

Your Sister and Your Father's Daughter

Notice is hereby given that this author claims the full trademark rights to the all inferences of the "Fiery Darts of the Assassin: Know the Nature of Your Enemy", the "Fiery Darts and Nature of Your Enemy" utilized throughout the various books, tapes and any and all electronic media used to convey the Fiery Darts of the Assassin: Know the Nature of Your Enemy Message.

© 2012, Patricia E. Adams

Copyright © 2012 by Patricia E. Adams

Printed and bound in the United States of America. All rights reserved. No part of this book may be reproduced or transmitted in any form or by any means, electronic or mechanical, including photocopying, recording, or by an information storage and retrieval system -- except by a reviewer who may quote brief passages in a review to be printed in a magazine or newspaper -- without permission in writing from the publisher. For information please contact Shekinah Publishing House, 877/538-1363. Although the author and publisher have made every effort to ensure the accuracy and completeness of information contained in this book, we assume no responsibility for errors, inaccuracies, omissions, or any inconsistency herein. Any slights of people, places, or organizations are unintentional.

Scripture quotations are from the KING JAMES VERSION of the Bible.
Printed in the United States of America

ISBN 09700976-9-7
LCCN 2004096312
Fiery Darts of the Assassin:
Know the Nature of the Enemy Satan

ATTENTION ORGANIZATIONS, HEALING CENTERS, AND SCHOOLS OF SPIRITUAL DEVELOPMENT:

Quantity discounts are available on bulk purchases of this book for educational purposes. Special books or book excerpts can also be created to fit specific needs. For information, please contact Shekinah Publishing, 1-877/538-1363.

Patricia E. Adams is a Christian, Speaker, Author, Mentor, Instructor, Coach, Leader, Children's Rights Advocate, Domestic Violence Advocate and Internet Radio Host.

She serves in her local church and community and a portion of her titles are series, one of which is called "The One Heart Series,' "The Set Free to Praise Him Series" and two upcoming series in development at this writing. She writes about the salvation journey as a process of becoming intimate with God.

There are 5 books currently in the One Heart Series; 1 in the Set Free to Praise Him Series and 4 additional titles. God has placed a strong gift of teaching within her that speaks the truth in love, with a commandment to draw his people out and into an intimate relationship with their God.

God has wrought a mighty deliverance in her life from the baggage of physical, sexual, emotional, and religious bondage. Her testimony is that God is a mighty Deliverer and Restorer. Patricia is available to share her testimony of deliverance and restoration to groups across the country and around the world.

Lectures/Seminars/Workshops/Keynotes
Writing & Publishing Seminars
Intellectual Property Workshops
Family Seminars (Men, Women and Children)
Ministry of Helps

Please contact her for additional information at
Email: author@oneheartseries.com
Radio Network: www.blogtalkradio.com/patricia-adams-live
Website: www.oneheartseries.com

This book is dedicated to those Preyed Upon -

Reflection

"Just because someone did not or does not love you the way that you think they should, doesn't mean they don't love you with all they have."

We all know someone, or have known someone or persons who have not loved us as we hoped they would. Whether they were biological, or intimate, or you were victimized by both. They only gave you what they had, but now it is time to move past what they did not have to give us and give ourselves what we deserve! Freedom from carrying around the dead weight of the people who have left us feeling empty and neglected and move into position to receive love from one who can love us to the maximum capacity of what we have made room to receive. Spring (deliverance) is in the air friends, in the natural and the spirit, while we spring clean our houses, garages and offices, how about the clutter in our souls. Just by faith, not by feeling release those who have hurt you in the past and the present from a debt they can not pay, the check you are waiting to cash will bounce anyway, because remember they can not give you what they don't have. Be free in the matchless and marvelous name of the lover of your soul Jesus Christ!" Again, may you find restoration and wholeness on every page for your life!

Your Sister in His Service Until He Shouts!

Table of Contents

Reflection xi
1- Set Free to Praise Him (Excerpt) 3
2- Scene of the Crime 43
3 - Aftershocks of Betrayal 65
4- Where Do We Go From Here? 91
5- Pursue as Leaders When God Says 99
6- Location, Location, Location 109
7- Let Us Esteem One Another 119
   Shadow 123
   Deception 124
   Armour of Light 125
   Abdication 126
   Submission 127
   Surrender 129
   Death 130
   Burial 131
   Resurrection 135
   Ascension 136
   Covenant 137
   Ring Giver 137
   Ring Maker 140
   Ring Wearer 143
   Reign 145
8- The Devil is a Liar 153
   God Hates - 156
   What About Satan 158
   Purpose 186
   An Armed Man 188
   Truthfulness: 188
   Breastplate of Righteousness 189
   Feet Shod 190
   Shield of Faith 191
   Helmet of Salvation 191

> Sword of the Spirit 192
> The Colicky Lust of the Flesh 193
> The Lust of the Eyes 195

Endnotes 215
Volumes in the One Heart Series 217
Other Books by Patricia E. Adams cont'd 219
Other Books by Patricia E. Adams cont'd 219

CHAPTER 1

Set Free to Praise Him Excerpt

1- Set Free to Praise Him (Excerpt)

Watershed according to Webster's Dictionary is when a crucial turning point affecting action, opinion, etc. is reached.

There is Popeye, Mighty Mouse and Underdog to emulate and hope that one of them works!

If I eat me's spinach I will be strong and able to take care of myself; or maybe I can be mild mannered and slip into a phone booth and change into Mighty Mouse and come out and save myself, oh well wait there is hope in Underdog, after all he is passive and yet invincible when messed with!

Well maybe not, but sure would be nice if my real parents showed up like that and saved the day! Daddy riding in on a white stallion and momma riding behind him on this white stallion racing towards where I am; and in any minute they are going to come and scoop me up and put me on the horse with them and we will ride away and never be found again! Wishful thinking! Can't blame a child!

These are my formative memories and this is who lives in the house where I use to live. There is a older man who lives in the house with us, but he sleeps in another room of the house, and I sleep in the bed with the older woman that I call my mother. And then there is a middle room and there is a younger woman sleeps in that room whenever she is home. There is another house that sits on the same land as ours but it is behind our house. Often I see the older man and the younger woman walking around this house. I remember being told by the older woman that the house was being built for the younger woman and was not finished! One day I remember asking the younger woman about her house and she did not answer me! But, somehow things just never seem to add up in my mind about the younger woman. Who is she? There is a younger boy that is older than me who frequents the house and he appears to be related to me. There are no pets that I can recall in or around the house where I use to live with my mother, her husband, and sometimes the young woman and the younger boy!

    Recollection of my life began as early as the age of two. One day I was lying in bed next to my mother drinking milk from a baby bottle around the age of two. I remember pulling the bottle out because it was empty and raising it up for more. My mother rose from beside me and took the bottle and called out to her husband to come and fill it with more milk. He came to the bedroom door and she rose to her feet to give him the bottle at the bedroom door. Suddenly, there is an argument and I become afraid because their voices are angry and loud.

    I recall him pushing past her and coming towards the bed where I was and he picked me up and began to walk out of the bedroom door with me. She reached out and snatched me out of his arms and threw me back on the bed and I began to cry. The argument continues and words were being spoken filled with accusations of him being out all night and of him having no right to touch me. She moves past him and toward the kitchen and just as quickly returned to my side with the bottle full of milk. He left the house and we lay back down.

Later that day I recall waking up and crawling down from the bed as she slept and I walked over to the dresser in the bedroom and began rambling in the drawers. I remember opening a compact and then picking up a round cream colored object with a nipple shape point in the center of the ring and I instinctively placed it in my mouth. By this time I had made so much noise she woke from her sleep and snatched the things away from me and began to fuss, but not at me for some reason.

There was a second door in the middle of our bedroom and she was facing the door and fussing at the door. She reaches for the door knob and opens the door and there is a young woman sitting at the foot of the bed in the room behind the door.

The young woman at the foot of the bed has her head held down and slowly looked up at her stepmother and never says a word while she's fussing at her. She's fussing about the compact and the cream colored object telling her that she had asked her to put them where I could not reach. I'm not sure how I understood the conversation about the cream colored object but it was the young woman's birth control ring that I had placed in my mouth. The young woman never said a word she got up from the bed and walked away. I walked into the room and stood at the foot of the bed and looked down where she had been sitting and saw the bed was soiled. I remember pointing it out to her stepmother and silence filled the room with the exception of the sound of the wind blowing against the blind on the window.

My next recall at age two is over to someone elses house and I am walking barefoot and it appears I am with people who know me, because my mothers husband is nearby. My mother never let me go barefoot! I am standing on the sidewalk and walking around the neighborhood. My feet are really hot I remember and I am scratching my head. A young girl catches up to me and puts a bracelet on my arm, and I look at it and ask her what it was. I could see letters on it but did not know what they said, she told me it was my name!

So I looked really hard at the letters and repeated after her as she called my name! It was pink and white and stretchy and it was mine! She went to touch it again and I snatched my arm away! It was mine! I am walking back to the front of this new place that I am at and a man has pulled up in front of the house and looks at me with a look that made me feel bad! I remember looking at myself and seeing my bare feet and my dress was pink but dirty and my diaper was hanging! He exchanged words with an older woman who was on the porch and looked at me again and then left! I remember looking down at the ground and scratching my head and looking down the street as he drove away. The whole time I had a feeling that he was somebody that I should have known but I did not, but I felt bad at the way he left me standing there on the sidewalk. But why?

My next recall is around age 3 and it is of the young woman who lived with us appears, and we are on a bus. I am sitting next to her in the seat and looking up at her! She is sitting next to the window, and people are talking to her and it appears about me, but she never responds to them to my recollection. We exit the bus and walk a few blocks to a house that seems to have long steps and inside of this house is an older woman with dark skin and a white dress on. She let's us in and the young woman walks me into this bedroom with a white covering on it and sets me down really hard on the covers and walks out into the hallway. I hear her telling the older woman that she could have me and the older woman is talking with her in a low voice and I cannot hear them anymore. I recall sitting on that white cover for a long time and falling asleep. The young woman has left me there with the older woman. Somehow, I end up with my mother and her husband coming for me at the older womans' house. I am unsure of how long after being left before they came for me. For some odd reason, this would happen again – where I was left with someone by the young woman.

By the time I am four, I have the next memory I have of this young woman is her outside the house cutting a birthday cake there a lot of children around playing in the yard. They are there for my birthday and it is my fourth birthday. While the other children are getting a piece of cake my mother takes me in the House and shows me a beautiful black baby grand piano course the size was for a child and that child was me. I must have let out a sound of excitement because the other children ran to the door of the house trying to get into see what all the excitement was about. I met them at the door and would not let them inside the house. It was mine and no one was going to play with my piano.

Mind you it was a child's version because I am only four years old at the time. A little girl rushes in the house past me to play with the piano and I tell her not to touch it and to leave the house. She is crying now and making a scene about not playing with my piano. Anyway the woman who brought me into the house took care of things. I know she did, because the little girl did not get to touch my piano. We are back outside and suddenly the party is almost over and I did not recall getting any cake or ice cream. The young woman at the end of the table is agitated and it seems to be with me for not sharing my piano.

  Oh well I think and the day seems to end after that. The women in this scene seem to be related to me. The older woman is who I call "Momma" and is who I grew to call my mother! The young woman is around for some reason, not sure why.

  My next memory of this young woman is during the winter my approximate age range is 4 years old and I had been allowed to go outside and play in the snow on the ground as long as I stayed near the porch. I began to play in the snow and I don't know why I looked up but I saw a car that looked familiar being driven by a man who was not and there were women in the back seat and one in the front seat. The closer the car came to our house I thought it would turn in the driveway but instead I heard laughter I called out to the young woman to come and see the familiar car she came to the porch and I looked up and I saw hole in her skirt in the the front under her blouse. The people in the car were laughing and I thought they were laughing at the young woman. Later, discovered they were laughing at both of us, but not for the reasons I had thought! The young woman appears to be happy to see the car driving up and becomes angry when the car slowly passes by with the man who wore a hat was pointing his finger out of the car towards us and laughing along with the sounds of the women in the car.

There was something familiar about this car, and I had seen the young woman driving this car without the man or the other people inside! I looked up at the young woman and she was in distress I felt embarrassed for her and myself and I did not know why. The familiar car turned the corner and they were all still laughing and pointing and the young woman was in hysterics.

My mother came to the door to see what was the matter and pulled her into the house and all I could hear was hysterics in the house. And I did not know who this man was, but he seemed familiar and the car seemed familiar with all of the laughing women in the car who had upset this young woman. But what I did know is that I did not like any of them and I didn't even know them, but they had upset the young woman that lived in the house with me, my mother and her husband very much!

I later learned from my mother that the hole in her skirt was not the reason they were laughing, the skirt was made that way. The young woman had been pregnant and I had never seen the young womans baby before! I did not see the young woman at the house for a while after that day!

My next memory of this young woman is of a group of children meeting in our yard all happy and lined up to take a trip to the corner store to buy treats. I have money and trying to figure out how far it will go when we get to the store. There are a whole lot of kids from the neighborhood and they are all following this young woman from the previous scene. She is leading the way and the children are happily following and I am pulling up the rear. She seems so happy – this young woman to be leading the children.

But wait am I not one of the children too, doesn't seem like it. Seems like I am an observer in this picture, there is a younger teen girl walking near me at the end of the line. I ask her about the older young woman we are following. Who is she I ask? The girl did not respond to my question to what I believe was my satisfaction. She called her Auntie. Well okay, whose Auntie and what is an Auntie anyway?

Well we keep heading for the store and I am really excited because there is so much to see. I watch the other kids pick what they wanted. I walked up to the counter and showed the man behind the counter how much money I had and asked him what I could buy. I am standing in from of a huge clear cookie jar with a red lid on it and the letters say "Tom's" – all I know is I want some of those big cookies with the funny looking man on them. Somebody called the cookies "Big Wheels" so I told the man behind the counter I wanted as many of those cookies as I could get, a bottle of soda, a dill pickle and some peppermints. He filled my bag full of cookies and asked me what soda I wanted and I told him a Coca-Cola. What a haul for those few coins I gave him, so I thought. Well I am happy as we are walking on the way back to the house behind the older young woman without ever saying a word to each other.

Another memory of older boys and one of them being related to me playing football in the yard. I am not so happy because the oldest neighbor boy is not playing football but sitting beside me on the porch as I a watching the other boys play football. The older neighbor boy is touching me and making me feel uncomfortable. I am four years old and he looks like a man to me in size sitting next to me. He tells me to be quiet and he seems nervous while touching me but he doesn't stop.

He is looking out to the yard and I looked out at the yard and the younger boys are still playing football and have not noticed what is going on with me. He tells me to get up and go into the house with him and he lays me down, places a pillow over my face and begins hurting me in my private part. I heard a loud noise suddenly while beneath the pillow and the pressure that was on me suddenly is gone too! My face is still under the pillow and I hear loud noises and I pull the pillow back to see that the younger boy has come to my rescue. The two of them are fighting all the way out of the house and into the front yard. I run out behind them and pick up a brick and try to hit the older neighbor boy and then I try to give it to the younger boy, and I am yelling and crying "kill him." Suddenly, the fighting stops and he does not kill him. But for some reason I feel safe.

Finally, somebody has looked out for me! For some reason that day seemed to only make me a target, because now the younger boys are rying to do things when I am alone. Walking down the street to the store or playing outside or sitting on the porch alone is no longer a place where I feel safe. I feel confused and unsure of who is going to be there to protect me. I am often at home alone for some reason. We have many businesses and they don't like having me around. But that soonc changes and I am at the place of business a lot that is nearest our house. There are a lot of grown people here and they are eating, drinking, dancing and playing cards. There is a huge place outback where smoke billows out of a huge black metal can that is as wide as the building. My mother's husband stands on top of wooden crates to stick a large fork in the meat and turn it over. I asked what that was and he said the word "Barbeque" and he my mothers husband seems to be cooking it most of the time. Inside the business there are people sitting on stools and ordering food, can drinks, and glass drinks and I want to help. We have someone in the back who cooks hamburgers and fries and all kinds of stuff and he does not say very much! My mother is giving directions and taking money and trying to keep me entertained.

There is music always playing and I want to know where it is coming from! So there is this big box with a glass face and it has round disc inside that drop and this metal arm moves on top and they start spinning. Then there is sound filling the room and people are dancing or talking louder. I want to dance, so I start dancing and people start throwing money at me on the floor. And kids are coming and standing at the door watching me dance. My mother is angry and she yells at the adults to stop throwing money at me, and she tells me to stop dancing!

I sense her frustration with my being there, but leaving me home alone is no longer an option. Until one day, there is a man yelling at my mother and I am angry about it and I run and pick up this huge knife and charge at the man with the knife. Fortunately, my mother grabs me and that is the day that she sends me home by way of her husband. He was suppose to stay there with me until time for them to close.

Well he left me there alone and the sounds of the house got the better of me and I run out of the house leaving the front door open and I am headed back to the place of business. I am almost there and a neighbor lady stops me and makes me stand next to the fence. She says I am going to call your momma, because you know you should not be out here walking. She asked where my mothers husband was, and I said I did not know!

She calls my mother and I can hear her talking loud and I know I am in some kinda trouble! The woman is not to let me move until she gets somebody to come and get me. I don't even remember who came and got me or where I ended up at that day! But I was in trouble, but not as much trouble as my mothers husband. When he left me at home alone, he did not return to the business, but went off somewhere else. He was so angry with me when he found out that I did not stay at the house like he told me to!

I recall the next day I am back at the place of business and being told to go make friends with some of the children in the houses near the place of business. I do and this is where I spend most of my time until the buiness closes for the evening. Playing in the neighborhood with the children and going inside of their houses to play with their toys and talk to their parents.

My next memory is of another younger woman about the age of the young woman who lives with us, who comes by to pick me up in a black four door car with a lot of other children inside of the car. She is really pretty just like the young woman that lives with us. Never hear them saying anything to each other when they are both around.

One day she picks me up and takes me over to her house where they live, which is not far from where we live and we are not there very long. Because the man who lives at her house is angry and we leave. We end up at the place of business and it is night time, and we don't get out and go inside, but there is a walk up window that you can go to. The older young woman has gotten out of the car and walked up to the window, because we are all hungry.

While she is at the window, the car starts to roll backwards with all of us childen inside and into the streets and we are all screaming.

About the time they notice the car we almost go backwards over the hill and onto the railroad tracks. An adult jumps in the car and stops it from going over the hill backwards and drives us back up to the parking lot at the business. I jump out and run inside to my mother and tell her what happened and a huge argument breaks out. I am left with my mother for the rest of the evening.

Then my next memory is of the young woman who lives with us laying on the living room couch telling me to go to the store and buy her cigarettes. I replied no and she threw a shoe at me and I ducked behind the chair. I stayed away from a her for a little while. Returned back and hid behind the chair and asked for permission to wash my hair. I am around the age of 5 years old she gives me permission to wash my hair. I go into the bathroom and lather my hair and turn on the water in the bathtub to rinse my hair out, but I get soap in my eyes and run to the young woman for help. She comes into the bathroom and begins to wash my hair.

    Suddenly she is no longer washing my hair but trying to drown me under the water faucet, I began screaming and trying to break away. Suddenly, I hear my mother and her husband coming to my rescue. They are pulling at the young woman to get her off of me, there are hysterics from everybody.

    Crying and angry words are being exchanged as I am sitting on the floor trying to catch my breath, and I am crying too! They stood in the hall arguing about what to do about the young woman for trying to drown me! I felt guilty because it was my fault she was in trouble I thought, if I had not asked her to wash my hair – this would have never happened. I don't see her anymore after that day! No one tells me where she is and I stop asking!

Now it is only my mother, her husband and myself who live in the house. I am still four, and one day I am passing through the middle bedroom where the young woman use to sleep. My mother yells at me to come out of her room. I told my mother I only wanted to go to the next room where her husband was. She told me to stay out of that room, and to go down the hallway to his room. I often go in and speak to him and sit on the floor and watch television with him.

He doesn't have anything to say to me. He seems to miss the young woman not being in the house, because he often stares out his bedroom window to the house that was never finished for her with sadness.

But, her husband always looks at me as if he is

angry at me, and I wonder why! But for some reason I am always left with him to go wherever he goes and my mother is at the business.

As I am walking through the hallway and mother is in the kitchen cooking and I stop to see if I can help her. She tells me no thank you and to go watch television. I head to the room where her husband sleeps and the television is on and I sit in the middle of the floor and just as I sit down. I see the man with a lot of hair and a woman with a hat in a car turning the corner, and suddenly a sound comes from the television that scares me. People are screaming and running on the television.

I am moving closer to the television and the car is coming up the street and I see blood coming from the man with the big head of hair and the woman with the hat is crawling out of the car. I hear someone say the President of the United States has been shot! I run screaming to the kitchen to my mother and tell her verbatim what I heard on the television. She doesn't believe me at first and she comes to see for herself and she starts crying! She asked her husband why did he let me see all of that and he had no response. I am not sure what happened that day other than there was a sadness in the house that made me sad!

There is another day where I am in the panel truck with mommas' husband and he has gone to some other local businesses to buy some things for our business and there were no seats in the truck. So, I sat on an empty white pickle bucket on the passengers side.

The side door began to open up and I told him about it, and he told me to grab hold to the door and pull it shut. I got up and grabbed the door and the truck sped up and I went flying out the door and landed on the side of the road. Fortunately, onto some grass and I was out like a light for a little bit, and when I came too I was still falling downward and a train was coming and I was almost to the train tracks.

Suddenly my arm reached from under me and I grabbed onto the blades of grass and dug my fingers into the side of the hill and stopped my fall. I climbed up the hill, dazed and bleeding and did not see my mothers husband anywhere. Just as I had reached the top of the hill I heard the train go by and blow its horn! I started walking towards the business and I could see the truck parked, and I wondered why he left me. The whole time I walked in pain my mind kept flashing back to his eyes!

I remember when I knew I was falling out of the truck I turned to him for help and I caught a glimpse of his eyes in the rear view mirror! There was that angry look in his eyes again, and I could not figure that out! Is that why he did not stop for me, because of the angry look in his eyes? I finally made it to the business, but another neighboring business owner had seen me walking and had called my mother at our business and told her that I was walking along the side of the highway.

As I was walking onto the parking lot of the business I can hear her talking and walking towards the door! They had been arguing about where I was, and I looked over at him and fainted! I never trusted him again after that!

My next recollection of him is that same year and it is still daytime and my mothers husband is playing with a snake he says and invites me to play with the snake too! I run out of his room screaming telling my mother that her husband is playing with a snake and he asked me to play with it too! She runs into the room and asks him about the snake and I am hiding behind her, and there is this huge argument. Then there is only my mother and me who live in the house. Her husband moves to the other house that belonged to the young woman. I see him all the time, but not allowed to go over to the other house very often by my mother.

Something awful happens soon aftter and we no longer live in this house, my mother and me.

We are in a new neighborhood and I am starting to school now. I am making friends in the new neighborhood and I am making new friends! I walk to school with the other children nearby and given instructions to come straight home. One day I did not come straight home and the young boy who use to live with us in the other house is sent to look for me!

I am on my way home when he and I meet up at the corner from where we now live and he grabs hold of me and is forcing me home. Yelling and telling me that I am going to get a whipping when I get home, because I should have been home long time ago. Where had I been? When I walked in the door I saw the look on my mothers face as she spun around from pacing the floor and she was mad! The whipping commenced and the explaining came later!

In this new neighborhood things were not quite the same for us, I still slept with my mother and the place was smaller. Her husband came through during the daytime and helped in the business at this address now! We no longer were at the other house or the other business as far as I can remember. We often went to another business we had in the same area to open and things were not quite the same there either! Something has happened and I am not sure, but I learn to adjust!

There is a neighborhood man who is mentally different who passes by the business when I am out front and talks to me as if he wants to be a friend. Mother sees him talking to me and she does not tell me to stop talking to him, so I think he is safe. One day the mentally different man comes by and he asks me to play arcades with him, as we have an arcade next door to our other business.

So I remember going inside and playing shuffleboard with him for a little while and then he wants me to go to the back of the arcade with him. I feel scared but, mother has never told me to be afraid of him; and that day I learned to be very afraid of him. Because that day he hurt me! I was left there while he walked away and told to not say anything to anyone about what happened! I could hear mother calling for me and I was afraid to say anything. When she came inside where I was and I was sitting on top of a table in the back room she asked me how I got there! I was unable to tell her what had happened because I was afraid that I had done something wrong. At some point I told her, but I don't remember how long it took me. Nothing happened to the man as far as I could tell because he kept walking the neighborhood, but not passing our part anymore!

I am about to turn six and I remember breaking my arm from being thrown off a see-saw and going to school the next day unable to write. Nobody knew that my arm was broken, I had been playing with the younger boy and his friends when this happened. Speedily, taken home crying and in pain – and he told mother what happened and she made me go to bed. She was still working.

The next morning I dressed and went to school and the teacher asked me why I was not writing and I told her I couldn't. She came over and looked at my arm and it was really big and sent me to the nurse, who called my mother to come and get me and take me to the doctors. I was six and my arm was broken and it was almost my seventh birthday!

The year before that I had broken my leg from climbing a tree and falling out when the neighbor yelled at me for climbing in her tree! I will never forget that her grandson came to my rescue to help me home! She was very mean to me and said very cruel things about me! Her grandson would take up for me, and he was about my age too I believe! Most of the recovery period from breaking my leg is a blur or when the cast came off!

I do know that my birthday was not too far away! As the day approaches my mother bought a pretty light blue chiffon dress with ruffles and put my hair in curls. She had to tear the sleeve of my dress to get it over my cast, and I was unhappy. Her husband had come by, because he did not live with us anymore! Since he was sitting in one of the chairs looking at me and hearing my mother argue about the cast being on my arm for my birthday! He told me to come there and he started cutting the cast off of my arm!

I guess to make her mad because it did, and when the cast came off my arm just dropped like a heavy rock to my side! He looked at my arm and said to my mother there was no swelling and I should be okay!

He told me that I would have to hold it up and work with it to get it back to normal. She threw the best parties, there was a long table from the wall to the door of the business she had decorated, and I had a huge cake and I had to blow out the candles on my cake and open presents and play with the other children until I was tired. My arm hurt really bad and my party had to be cut short, because I had to lay down.

I remember later that same year of being stung by a nest of bees and having to be rushed to the hospital! The doctor said to me that I needed to stop coming to the hospital so much! I was a tom-boy! He told my mother and her husband that I was severely allergic to them and they should take precautions that I not get stung anymore anytime soon! She just looked at me, knowing that I was always into something!

But I heard the doctor and I was extra careful around the bees after that. Later that day the young boy who lived with us at the other house shows up and I show him the cast and I take him to where I had been stung, and he sat the hive on fire! I felt safe and again he was my hero!

A few months later it is still warm and I am playing around with the juke box and I will never forget this song. It was by Junior Walker and the words said something about shot gun – shoot him fore he run now! And I made up a dance to go to the song and was in the middle of the floor dancing, and people had started to come in to eat and drink. They were throwing money at me and she yelled at me and them to stop! The next thing I recall that day is trying to be a help to my mother! I had learned how to stand on a wood crate and boost myself up to the grill to cook hamburgers and pork chops when she was not looking. The person who was on the grill would let me whenever she was not watching. Well I got chased away from the grill so, I decided to come and help behind the counter. We used block ice and an ice pick to break the ice up for drinks.

Somebody asked for some ice and before my mother knew it, I had grabbed the ice pick and went to chopping. I was doing pretty good, and the next jab went straight into my finger and I raised my hand up to her with the ice pick still in it and boy was I in pain. I did not cry until she took out as she almost fainted at the sight. She dressed it up and made me get out from behind the counter. I had to go to bed and there is where I headed. There were so many things that would happen that I guess you could say were part of growing up and a lot of other things that should not have been part of growing up! My next attempt at helping out was with a coffee urn and trying to pour somebody a cup of coffee. Did not realize I knew how to turn it on but not how to turn the faucet off! That hot coffee kept coming and I ended up with severe burns on both of my arms, and back to the hospital I went!

That was a very painful experience and I still have them to remind me of that day! My best memories of my mother dressing me up like a cute little girl in pinks and blues and reds and taking very good care of me and my hair! She took me to church until the pastor rejected me for a role in the Easter Play! We never went back to church after that, and she fussed about it for a long time! I read the part from the Bible very well, it was his personal decision to choose another little girl! My mother never got over that! It was years later that I found out why!

We went home and she stayed upset most of that day! The next encounter I had with a snake was when one was curled underneath the juke box and my mother had managed to climb on top of the juke box for safety. I had just opened the door and she yelled to me not to come in!

She told me that there was a snake inside and it had crawled underneath the juke box and to go and get help!

I ran to the business next door and no one was there, and I ran to the first house on the corner and the man there grabbed a black bar from a chest on his porch and ran towards the business. I ran behind him and he told me to stay back, he went and saw my mother still on top of the juke box!

He killed that snake somehow with that black bar and took it out the back door! My mother climbed down and she is really shook up and I don't leave her side for the rest of the day! But there was something strange about that day and that snake being underneath the jukebox! The room was very tense for awhile! My mommas' husband shows up later that day and she is telling him about the snake and he does not have very much to say about any of it. She asks him to go do something and to take me with him, and I look at her funny! She told him that he needed to come straight back with me! Well what he did do was take me by a house not too far from where we were and leave me in the truck with the windows up! He walks up to this yellow house and climbs the stairs and knocks on the door and a woman comes to the door and greets him and he goes inside and stays for awhile.

When he comes back to the truck I am hot and thirsty and a little bit confused, but not too confused! He made me sware not to say anything to my momma!

Remember, this is my momma he is talking about and I know for a fact he does not really care for me or my momma! What do you think happened when we got back! You got it! I told my momma and all kinds of words got to flying that day! He looked at me with the look he usually looked at me with and I just looked back. Remembering now how he left me when I fell out of the truck and how he had asked me to play with a snake, that wasn't really a snake!

From that day forward whatever my momma told me to do in regards to him, that is what I did! One day he had been out the whole weekend and he chose to stop by and see us and he sat in the booth and fell asleep! She told me to go and get the hot sauce and shake it down his throat while he was sleep! And I did, and when he woke up – wow what a time that was! I didn't get in trouble, but the tension between us had grown by then – that it really did not matter anymore – how he felt about me! Momma plans a trip for us to go and visit the young woman who used to live with us and it is near her birthday! She begins to try and explain why we are going to see her and that I should use my allowance to buy her a present. I was told what she liked and I went to the downtown drugstore with my momma's husband and bought three things and put a bow on the package for this young woman! We drive to see the young woman and momma sets up a picnic on the lawn and there are some other children around too! She tells me to go with her husband to see the young woman and I walk with him to see her with my opened gift. That one of my cousins had opened and used knowing it was for the young woman! I was angry, but I was sure the young woman would not hold that against me!

We walk down the long walk way and into the waiting room. My mommas husband told me to sit on the opposite side of the room and he would sit nearest the door! She came around the corner and saw him and me and she sat opposite of both of us. He asked her to go for a walk with us and join us for the picnic! We walked outside and he is telling her that I brought her a present, and he said look your baby brought you a gift! And at that very moment she turned to look at me and said that is not my baby and don't ever bring her back! I burst into tears and ran as fast as I could to mommas arms! Sobbing and tyring to tell her what she had said to me! My momma's husband lingered behind with the young woman that lived with us sometimes! By the time he reached the picnic area, momma was packing it in and telling him she knew it was not a good idea!

We left and I was in distress and questions ran through my mind! Why would she say something so hurtful to me, and why was it that I was her baby! I had a momma, was it just a form of expression! Anyway, I didn't need her because I had a momma, and I did not care if I ever saw her again after that day!

It was not many days after that - that my life got really bad!

CHAPTER 2
Scene of the Crime

Scene of the Crime

2- Scene of the Crime

Who knew that the day was about to turn black and the sparkle in my eyes would dim on such a day that was so nice outside that the front door is open and the screen is unlatched. All signs to a little girl that all is well, she is safe in the world ! When I am at my Aunties sometimes she would let us take a portable television and a pallet and sleep outside in the front yard under the stars! This day was not too hot to be outside playing if I had not eaten that stupid piece of chocolate candy from the refrigerator last night!

My cousins played a trick on me and told me that it was chocolate candy, why are my cousins laughing about me eating this chocolate candy? Maybe because my Auntie is going to be mad and I am going to get in trouble?

I ate all of that candy in that little blue box, at least that was what I thought I was eating! Boy was I going to be in big trouble when my Auntie found out! Instead during the night it made my stomache upset and queasy and the other end of me; well you know the rest! My cousins who were laughing the day before are angry because they have to clean up after me! Why must they play tricks on me like that? Always trying to get me to eat stuff that will make me sick!

Really is only the beginning of how my day would make my stomache turn inside out!

The year is 1966, all cleaned up and still can't go outside because my stomache keeps growling so loud you can hear it through the whole house! They are always playing dumb tricks! Oh well, the music is playing and I love to dance, so I will just dance at the top of the stairs to be near the restroom!

The radio is on and the radio station is playing all of my favorites! The DJ is Rudy V and it is the station 'we' listen to.

The DJ stops the music and there is silence! I rush to the radio to turn up the sound thinking it was broken or something. Now the phone is ringing downstairs, my Auntie is talking and I hear her to tell my older cousins to turn the radio off. But before they can the DJ begins to make the announcement that would change an already tumultous life into a Tsunami! He begins to say that there has been a horrible crime committed on one of the local business owners. He asks the community to please donate blood as she has lost a lot of blood! He tells the name of the neighborhod, and the name sounds familiar to me, and I have not yet made the connection, and then he says the name of the business and my mind begins to make the connection, and then he begins to tell what happened to the business owner and that by the time she had been discovered she had lost over half of her blood and was presumed dead! He said the name of the business owner, and that name sent an energy through my face that made the whole world seem to close in on me! He said my mommas' name and then I screamed!!!

My Auntie is yelling and saying to my cousins I told you to turn the radio off, so she would not hear! They were frozen in place behind me! Then the hustle to get out of the house begins and I am being told to stay behind and I am screaming and running down the stairs! Hollering I am not staying behind and I want to see my momma!!!! Stop it! I am going…you are not leaving me here…who said I couldn't go…that's my momma….get out of the way!!!! @#$

They give in and the ride to the place of business with me in tow is underway! We pull up and there are cars everywhere and people and police and an ambulance backed up to the door of the business! They are trying to keep me in the car and I bolt out! The police had been looking for me because I was listed as unacounted for, I remember. Always, always we were never apart, but this weekend she had insisted I go to visit my Auntie! Why???? Had I been there I could have protected her!

The police are talking to people around and my Auntie, my mommas' sister and my mommas' husband! They told me to stay out and when I kept yelling at them to move out of my way...move…let me in!!!!!!@#$

The smell in the place is different, what is that smell? It is so strong and it is taking my breath away, the room feels like it is a loud thumping heart beat, and the air is moist, the odor is drawing me to a place in the room! I am drawn closer and I see blood running down the drain of the floor through the grids and then the white outline around the size of my mommas body and an iron on the floor, and our cash register on the floor, the ironing board is turned over and the room is a mess! My mind is overloaded and I take off running out the back door and down the street away from the business! Running and breathing hard and looking at all of the houses on the street and wondering why no one seems to be outside! I am at the end of the street now and nowhere else to run, so I sit down on my usual curb and a neighborhood boy comes over to me and started talking to me and I told him to go away, because I needed to think!

I looked back behind me at the house that was above the curb, and I get to my feet and run to the side door where I always went to when I wanted to play with her children! She answered and saw that I was crying, and she said she heard about what happened to my momma and she was sorry! I asked her if I could live with her and her children because I had no place to go!

She said to me you know I can't do that and you will have someplace to go and closed the door! I walked away with my head down, did she not get it!

My momma is dead and her husband is not going to want to keep me and my auntie has her own children, and I have nobody! I started to walk back up the street towards the business and I refused to go back through the back door or the front door, I stood at the corner of the building and watched the ambulance pull off and I waited for it to go away!

Who would nurture my heart now and keep me safe?

My momma's husband does not say anything memorable to me the whole time or console me in anyway that I can recall! There is no concept of time or days for me, just sunsets and sunrises! People are bustling about and I don't have a clue what's going on and nobody is bothering to tell me anything! I am left to my own devices! I spend time wandering around the neighborhood and playing in the neighboring yards and children seem to avoid me, I am sitting down on the neighbors porches until they tell me to leave.

Not sure why I did that? One day I came inside the house during the daylight hours and for some reason there was a stack of mattresses almost up to the ceiling wrapped in plastic and I loved to climb trees, so they became my mountain! I would climb up to the very top and lay down and begin to cry and cry and cry; until somebody would yell at me to shut up!

And sometimes I would shut up and other times I would tell them to shut up! My auntie comes to me and ask me to come down from my mattress mountain, and ask me if I want to go to the Hospital and see my momma? I said I thought she was dead! She told me that people heard the request for blood and came and donated blood for her so that by the time she got to the hospital they were able to help her! No one had told me!!!!

They pull out a dress for me to wear and shoes and comb my hair and take me to the hospital! I am trembling and afraid to see a dead woman, so I thought! They sent a nurse in to talk to me in a separate room before they brought me in. She told me some bad things, but that I needed to be strong for her, because her heart was weak and she wants to see me! The nurse walks away and my Auntie comes in and ask me if I am ready to go see my momma! And I said no, I leaned against the warm radiator because it was cold in that place!

She takes my hand anyway and pulls me towards the door of the empty room they had placed me in to calm me down. I walk toward the door of my mommas hospital room with my Auntie blocking my view, and suddenly she moves and I am standing by myself and she is reaching her arms out towards me. She has all kinds of things on her arm, and I don't look any further than her arm for a while.

I looked to the left and her sister was sitting next to her bed and there were other people in the room standing around and she calls my name "Patricia" and I look back at her and it is then when I see her face for the first time! I screamed, and she began to cry and they rushed me out of the room! Fussing at me and telling me to stop screaming! I screamed because her face was disfigured from the beautiful face I had known!

What happened to her face I asked, what happened to her face! The nurse did not do a good job preparing me for what I saw, it frightened me!

She was a light complexioned woman and there were dark brown marks all over her face like a waffle pattern. The spots reminded me of waffles and the grid of the waffle iron! My auntie said it was because the man who attacked her burned her in the face with the pressing iron! My mind went back to the scene of the crime where I had seen the iron on the floor next to the outline of her body! That's why it was down there, I thought and that is why the ironing board was turned over! My mind thought did he try to press her face on the ironing board!

I asked why would he do something like that to her? They had to begin to tell me the truth! He had entered the place of business under the pretense of needing change to ride the bus. It was the beginning of the business day when he came in and the front door was open as she was preparing to open. She had been ironing the red checkered table cloths when he came in and asked her for change! She went to give him the change and that is when he attacked her.

They told me all of the gruesome details much to my dismay! He choked her with the ironing cord until she passed out and then began to beat her with the iron and burn her face with the hot iron! He took the brass cash register off the counter and took the money out, but also chose to beat her in the head with the cash register too! He left her for dead because he thought she was dead and that day…the day that she insisted that I be somewhere else was the day I would have physically died too! nstead I became the living dead! I was still dead inside! I had already experienced more than enough to stop me from being a child of innocence! But on top of that the little girl in me stopped smiling and stopped seeing the world as a nice place to be for a child! The photo above of me playing a cheerleader for the older kids who are playing street football are my cousins and my mommas' husband four months before my birthday! She threw the best birthday parties and that would be the last, because one month later she was left for dead!

Time lapsed for me during those days, she was officially dead four months after my birthday and three months after the attack. Then comes the final farewell, I never went back to the hospital before she died, because she was already dead in my heart!

We are at the church and there is the pink box at the front of the church and the church is packed with people and I am dressed up and standing by someone and there is crying and I start crying!

The preacher is in the pulpit and he is saying things and I am restless and I want to leave! What are we doing here and why are all of these people looking at me?

They manage to calm me down for a little while, until they open the pink box at the front of the church!

I look from the row I am on and see them uncover what was inside the box and I remember seeing the wavy black head of hair and then a face! I know that face, is that my momma, and I turn around and ask what is she doing up there in that box and then I see people moving towards the box. I want to know what those people are doing going towards my momma, and why is my momma in that pink box at the front of the church and why is nobody answering me!

Suddenly, people that I recognize start moving towards my momma, and I am calling out their names and they just look at me and keep walking. Then there are two men who begin moving the pink box toward the front row and I see more people that I recognize and some of them are my mommas' sisters, and my mommas husband, my auntie has my hand and she walks me towards the pink box. I touch the pink box and it feels like bumpy velvet and cold metal! I smell flowers and I look up and see the flowers on the end of the pink box, and people are blocking my view. Suddenly, I can see now and my momma is in this pink box and not moving and I froze and they tried to push me towards her and I would not budge.

I ran away from them towards the back of the church and I wanted to run out of the doors, but where would I go? I could hear people saying poor girl as I ran past them! Why are they saying poor girl? I run as far as the back window of the church and I stand and look back at the front of the church and people are still sitting down.

Then the pink box starts down the aisle and I am terrified as it is coming towards me, but I cannot move! Someone comes and takes my hand and my next recollection is of being in a black car with a lot of other people, and my screaming and crying "I want my momma" to the top of my lungs! My mommas' husband most memorable words that day; were not spoken to me but to the people in the car "make her shut up." There is someones hand who covers my mouth and my eyes are bulging as I am staring out the front window of the car we are in at the pink box in front of us inside another black car.

I was screaming into their hand and looking at him and he (my momma's husband) sat there with his hands in his lap! We are at the cemetery and we put the pink box in the ground and for all I cared they could have put me in there too, because I was truly dead inside! My momma's husband which I am sure you all are wondering why I am not saying my father by now. Well there must be a reason for that which you will find in a few!

Who are these people and what is to become of me is running through my mind!

No one had come to claim me and I knew that my momma's husband did not want to keep me, so who was going to have me next!

Please note that my definition of mother is not the one who gives you birth but the one who does the mothering to your heart! I had now lost a second woman in my life and my only momma! My hero who nurtured my heart was now gone forever!

How many mothers does a child get to have in life? For me she was my first and my last! There would be many other women in my life who have desired to be called mother by me, but none like her! There are those who are in my Mothers' Hall of Fame because they nurtured my adult heart! From that day a feeling of detachment and caution surrounded me and what minimal protection from taboo lines being crossed in my life were totally gone and the taboo lines got crossed often! Who would nurture my heart and who would guide and protect me now in this world I had not learned to navigate!

The lines were being crossed before she died but not without repercussions and that made it easire to take when the lines were crossed.

But now I knew there would be no repercussions when the lines were crossed from that day forward! Lord why didn't I die too? I am seven and I have no mother or father! Am I jinxed?

Who will take care of me at least as well as mother had?

The being passed from one place to the other begins! Nobody has room in their home for me! My mothers' husbands parience for my being around him is wearing thin! And the next thing I remember is being downtown at a second hand clothing store getting a new set of gently used clothes! Never before had I wore somebody elses clothes! Where were my clothes, all I had on were a pair of cut off denim shorts and a top and shoes! Why did I need to have someone elses clothes? My mothers' husband comes with the bags and we head to the truck and I am in tow!

    He takes me to a familiar place and leaves me with them for a while and they have expressed they cannnot keep me because they have their own kids! Days go by and he comes back and picks me up and takes me somewhere else! That somewhere else was a place that came as close to entering hell as I will ever want to encounter. The most supreme betrayal was underfoot, separated from all I knew and taken to a place that I did not know to be with people I did not know or understand! He took me to them in exchange for $10,000.00 which they never paid to him and then he enlist the aide of the court to get me back and they get their lawyer and the battle for custody ensues! Getting past the betrayal when there are no answers and the world is not making sense for me, in a moment no mother, no brother, no home and my clothes are gone. With that I stand at the front door of this house in tennis shoes, cut-off jean shorts, a sleeveless top and a bag of green grapes! Ushered into the front door staring at the woman who answered the door and looking at the inside of this house. It was a very nice house, but I could already sense it was a cold and sterile place in comparison to where I came from! How long was I to be here I asked him? He said two weeks! Okay, I said I can do this for two weeks and at the end of two weeks I was still nursing the green grapes and the same clothes and went out on the front porch and sat down and waited and waited and waited! Well, nightfall came and he never shows up until he realizes he has been deceived into believing he was going to collect the $10,000.00! Well how do you move past the initial trauma of the crime scene and the tremendous loss to being in a matter of months reassigned if you would into the hands of people whose favorite quote was "I'll straighten you out if I have to put you in a hat box to do it" – what did that mean! Well you can only imagine in my mind when I was being beaten with whatever was handy to the point of drawing blood; that it crossed my mind is that what it meant to be in a hat box! Aftershocks and tremors and flashbacks ahead oh my!

CHAPTER 3
Aftershocks Of Betrayal

3 - Aftershocks of Betrayal

Being added to the aftershocks and tremors and flashbacks come the objectivity as a sexual object. Being an object is being denied recognition of your existence as a living person with emotions and feelings of their own. Sexual objectification is always bad because it takes the dignity of that human person, whether it is a man or woman, and make it into an object or something subhuman.

Bob Gass, says that all of us have chapters we wish we could rewrite. And that Dr Harold Bloomfield says, 'Unresolved emotional pain wreaks havoc on your immune system, cardiac function, hormone levels, and other physical functions. We must make peace with our past because our life may literally depend on it.' To get over your past you must, first start looking at it differently.

Reframe it. Ask, 'How did it make me stronger? What do I know now that I didn't know then?' Don't focus on what you lost, but on what you gained.

Second, understand the difference between guilt and shame. Guilt is feeling bad about what you've done - it's healthy; shame is feeling bad about who you are - it's toxic and debilitating, but when God created us He said, '… it was very good… ' (Gen. 1:31 NKJV), start seeing yourself as He sees you.

Third, stop punishing yourself with the 'if only's'. After stumbling badly and having God pick him up, David wrote, 'Happy is the person whose sins are forgiven… whom the Lord does not consider guilty… ' (Psalm 32:1-2 NCV).

Forgive yourself; God has. Because He sees you through the cross, you are 'accepted' (Ephesians 1:6 NKJV). Finally, move from pain to gain. Healing takes time, so expect some anger, fear and sadness. Don't disown them; they're part of the process. But don't adopt them either; know when it's time to move on. You can't walk backwards into the future, and the future God has in mind contains more happiness than any past you can remember.

"...After all, "God said, let us make man in our image, after our likeness…" Adam's life was in God, and God was in Adam. When the life force of God touches us or things around us there is an outward sign..." How do you recognize when it is time to let go and what is it that you are letting go of?

The Object Seen As A Toy

An object for children to play with. Something of little importance; a trifle. An amusement; a pastime: thought of the business as a toy. A diminutive thing or person. To amuse oneself idly; trifle: a cat toying with a mouse. To treat something casually or without seriousness.

The American Heritage® Dictionary of the English Language, Fourth Edition copyright ©2000 by

Houghton Mifflin Company. Updated in 2009. Published by Houghton Mifflin Company. All rights reserved.

The Object Alienated

Alienation, for Marx, is the estrangement of humans from aspects of their human nature. Since - as we have seen - human nature consists in a particular set of vital drives and tendencies, whose exercise constitutes flourishing, alienation is a condition wherein these drives and tendencies are stunted. The opposite of, alienation is 'actualisation' or 'self-activity' - the activity of the self, controlled by and for the self.

We hold these truths to be self-evident, that all men are created equal, that they are endowed by their Creator with certain unalienable Rights, that among these are Life, Liberty and the pursuit of Happiness. "

U S Declaration of Independence 1776

...recognition of the inherent dignity and of the equal and inalienable rights of all members of the human family is the foundation of freedom, justice and peace in the world "

Preamble to the Universal Declaration of Human Rights, 1948

Children's Rights

Are the perceived human rights of children with particular attention to the rights of special protection and care afforded to the young,[1] including their right to association with both biological parents, human identity as well as the basic needs for food, universal state-paid education, health care and criminal laws appropriate for the age and development of the child.[2] Interpretations of children's rights range from allowing children the capacity for autonomous action to the enforcement of children being physically, mentally and emotionally free from abuse, though what constitutes "abuse" is a matter of debate. Other definitions include the rights to care and nurturing.

Types of rights

Children's rights are defined in numerous ways, including a wide spectrum of civil, cultural, economic, social and political rights. Rights tend to be of two general types: those advocating for children as autonomous persons under the law and those placing a claim on society for protection from harms perpetrated on children because of their dependency.

These have been labeled as the right of empowerment and as the right to protection. One Canadian organization categorizes children's rights into three categories:

1. **Provision:** Children have the right to an adequate standard of living, health care, education and services, and to play. These include a balanced diet, a warm bed to sleep in, and access to schooling.

2. **Protection:** Children have the right to protection from abuse, neglect, exploitation and discrimination. This includes the right to safe places for children to play; constructive child rearing behavior, and acknowledgment of the evolving capacities of children.
3. **Participation:** Children have the right to participate in communities and have programs and services for themselves. This includes children's involvement in libraries and community programs, youth voice activities, and involving children as decision-makers

In a similar fashion, the Child Rights Information Network, or CRIN for short, categorizes rights into two groups:

1. **Economic, social and cultural rights**, related to the conditions necessary to meet basic human needs such as food, shelter, education, health care, and gainful employment. Included are rights to education, adequate housing, food, water, the highest attainable standard of health, the right to work and

rights at work, as well as the cultural rights of minorities and indigenous peoples.

2. **Environmental, cultural and developmental rights**, which are sometimes called "third generation rights," and including the right to live in safe and healthy environments and that groups of people have the right to cultural, political, and economic development.

When your rights are violated as a child you experience an ultimate form of betrayal! And P. Bunny Wilson says that betrayal has a baby and that the baby's name is bitterness!

Betrayal happens to all of as we walk through life, but it requires relationships to fully be realized to its depth. Nobody really feels betrayal like someone who has been in a relationship with someone who betrays them through lies, failure to live up to commitments and to act nobly towards you! Broken trust is a result of things that come at us from unexpected directions and from people we have come to expect more from!

How do you trust again and how do you redeem the value of the relationship that has been broken?

To betray someone often requires forethought and a conscious decision to walk away from a relationship. It is focused on the individuals needs and not the needs of the relationship! Most often betrayal will come from those closest to you and it leaves the most detrimental path of destruction before, during and after the betrayal! Have you been betrayed by someone you trusted? We then turn to ways of healing the hurt and oftentimes we begin to practice ways of self-preservation.

The need for self-presevation to the degree that we risk the loss of face and relationships with others. Sometimes we even want to know what is in it for us if we have not truly healed from betrayal and our vision is narrowed so that we cannot see how our decisions will affect us or others!

Betrayal is a common occurrence throughout the course of history and it finds its place in the pages of the most sacred book most of us own, "The Bible"!

When Jesus was betrayed by Judas, how did he respond to the betrayal? Even though he was God in the flesh, Jesus still had to contend with his flesh. And be certain flesh will always wants to remain the victim. Since, Jesus was human it would not have been beneath him to feel victimized and to behave as a victim! It was within the scope of his human existence! But the price for playing the victim card would have not allowed him to past the test so that you and I would be empowered to lay down the victim card! Had he chosen to be the victim you and I would not have the possibility of being victors and victorious!

Learning from betrayal; some of us learn to grow up in Christ and make quality choices. While others of never learn how to respond to what has been done to us in a healthly manner.

We cannot see our problems facing us with any type of solution and we become problematic in nature! This leads to problematic relationships and a skewered perception of the world and we carry this problematic presence into every environment that we enter! People hate to see us coming because the atmosphere changes as soon as we enter the room! This is what the enemy has done to prevent you from being connected and in relationships. May you make a conscious decision to take back your God given power and authority restored by Jesus Christ!   Before accepting Christ into my life my dominion had been weakened, trampled on and misued by those who were in authority over me! The choice was mine to stay the victim and allow the living and the dead to continue to rule over me long after the grave had closed! This ends the excerpt from Set Free to Praise Him: From the Hand of the Saboteur into the Hands of God, ISBN: 9780970097651

Below are some types of spiritual conflicts that attach themselves to us as a result of the highlighted categories and that Satan uses as darts to attack us.

SEXUAL SINS
Fornication
Adultery
Pornography
Bestiality
Incest
Lust (fantasies)
Masturbation
Homosexuality
Rape
Exhibitionism

DRUGS
Illegal (name the drug):
Legal (name the drug):
Alcohol
Nicotine

IDOLATRY
Eastern religions (name):
Meditation -
Chanting,
Mantras,
Invocations
Cults (name them):
Secret Orders (name):
Material things (name):
People (name):

OCCULT PRACTICES
Astrology
Fortune telling or Tarot cards
Ouija Board
ESP
Séances
Hypnotism
Out of Body experiences
Witchcraft, Satan worship
Mind Control
Psychic healing
Dungeons and Dragons
ESP
Other (name):

FEAR
Worry
Anxiety
Depression
Hopelessness

UNBELIEF
Doubts
Lack of trust

ANGER
Towards God
Towards Self
Towards Parents
Towards others (name):
Bitterness
Hatred
Revenge
Unforgiveness

ENVY
Covetousness
Jealousy
Rebellion - towards authority

PRIDE
Self-centeredness
Poor self-image
Self-sufficiency

LIES
Believing Satan's lies
Lack of honesty
Deceitfulness

STEALING
Gambling

CURSING
Blasphemy
Slander
Gossip

VIOLENT ACTS
Attempted suicide
Abortion
Rape
Fighting
Beating others up
Planning how to harm others

SATANISM
Bargain with Satan
Worship of Satan

MUSIC
Occultist
Satanic

SPELLS & CURSES
Anything else you feel guilty of

CHAPTER 4
Where Do We Go From Here?

CHAPTER 4
Where
Do We
Go
From Here?

4- Where Do We Go From Here?

The Assassin; Satan comes to steal, kill and destroy the potential opportunity for an individual to return to the arms of the heavenly father and walk in the divine plan he has laid out before the foundation of the world for their life! Obstruction from believing on the name of the Lord God requires individual and corporate participation from mankind with Satan. We are waging war in the heavenlies while on this earth!

What is this war like? It is an organized conflict between good and evil, righteousness and unrighteousness. Between countries, political groups or religious groups.

Why do we wage war? It is to gain CONTROL! Control of spiritual territory, physical land or the government or to kill as many of the enemy as possible. It is a form of competition that may be face-to-face or predatory.

How do we obtain the victory? Do we accept that we have come to a standoff and there will be no real victory at this campaign and live to fight another day! Or we come into a place of submission to prevent destruction, or we completely destroy the enemy!

- **<u>KEY: Warfare is rooted in DECEPTION!</u>**

All of the fiery darts that the enemy has sent or sends your way as derailments, as ambushments and as threats of annihilation must be addressed!

Why must we wage war in the heavenlies? In order to kill the enemy you must become holy and righteously incensed or angry at what the enemy meant for evil over your life! You must be willing to stand up full of the spirit that is trained on the word of God. We must become disciplined in every area and level of our lives. Spirit, soul, mind and body! We must make a very clear and conscious effort to live healthy lives spiritually, emotionally, mentally and physically! Who can wage war if we are out of balance!

DECEPTION is rooted in FEAR! Fear of what? Fear of failure or success! Most of us thing we are afraid of failure, but it is the fear of success that takes the upperhand! And this is where the enemy will set in with the derailments! He will send things in your path that are customized to your bend, our iniquities and generational pattern. If your people were known for certain weaknesses then the enemy will make sure that there is an opportunity to entrap you with that weakness. Scripture tells us that let no man say that when he is tempted, that he is tempted of God!

James 1:13 Let no man say... I am tempted by God. Some men when they fall try to throw the blame on God, as if God had tempted them. It is impossible that God be tempted of sin, nor does he ever tempt men to sin. (People's New Testament)

In Psalms 32:5 David said,

"Then I acknowledged my sin to you and did not cover up my *iniquity*. I said, "I will confess my *transgressions* to the LORD"--and you forgave the guilt of my sin. Selah"

What is iniquity? It is fault, iniquity, mischief, punishment of iniquity and sin. In II Kings 7:9; Psalm 51:5; Psalm 51:7 the word iniquity relates to perversity, evil morals, fault, mischeif, punishment (of iniquity) and sin.

What is transgressions? Rebellion, breach of trust rebellious and rebellious act(s). Now in what ways do you know of your family being taken in iniquity and transgressions, and think of how they have either been ensnared or overcome them! If you see more have been ensared than have overcome then this has become a curse and possibly a stronghold over your families blood line!

How many generations of men and women have been ensnared, how many people have not completed a mission or purpose for their lives.

What are your families natural abilities and spiritual giftings? How many of them have fulfilled or are currently utilizing them to their fullest capacity?

How many people in your family have become incarcerated? How many people in your family have died premature deaths? How many people in your family have died violently? How many people in your family have not completed their education? How many people in your family have conceived children outside of marriage? How many people in your family have had stable or unstable marriages? How many people in your family have been preyed on by predators? Count them, maybe you have none of this and maybe everywhere you look you see evidence of the iniquities and transgressions of the generations!

Are you irritated, are you angry are you roused to want to make a change in your generation!

Then this is godly anger and it is the kind of anger that will not cause you to send but to take action! What action is there to take? To become disciples of the Most High God is a great place to start if you have not already done so! If you are a believer and these things are still going on then this is a good place to take a stand, like Shammah! Shammah a Harodite, took a stand in II Samuel 23:12 "But he took his stand in the midst of the plot, defended it and struck the Philistines; and the LORD brought about a great victory."

Let's look at what Shammah the Harodite did.

- He **took** a stand

    Where did he take his stand?

- In the midst of the plot

    What did he do in the midst?

- He defended it. (He went on the offense)

    When he did, what happened?

- He struck the enemy of his destiny

What happened after he struck his enemy

- The LORD brought him victory!

    o **GREAT Victory!**

CHAPTER 5
Pursue as Leaders When God Says

5- Pursue as Leaders When God Says

Shammah a Harodite (Hararite - Interpreted to mean "mountaineer," one from the hill country of Judah or Ephraim) displayed his righteous indignation and anger at what the enemy was doing through the Philistines and he determined that there was an advantage from defeating the enemy! He did not go to battle for the sake of waging war, he knew there were spoils and rewards to be had!

As a leader amongst his people who knew the fate of his family was in his hands. He knew that his decision was going to determine whether his people would obtain peace or be in peril based on his choice.

In II Samuel 23:11 fear had struck his people,

"Now after him(David) was Shammah the son of Agee a Hararite. And the Philistines were gathered into a troop where there was a plot of ground full of lentils, and the people fled from the Philistines." David had routed the Philistines until his hand cleaved to his sword (he had a cramp in his hand and it would not release the sword) but Shammah came after him to finish the job and secure the produce of their land.

Seeing that David had become weakened in battle after slaying so many of the enemy, he discerned with his spirit and observed with his eyes that they must be finished off! This was a quality decision that flowed with the anointing of David his leader, and just as God had given David a Great Victory, Shammah was assured the same outcome. So, in the next verse he takes a stand to secure the land and to prevent his people from perishing!

Once he took his stand then he implemented a strategy! He could not wage war with talking to them at this point, because it appears they were past the talking point! The only option he had was face-to-face confrontation! And in that confrontation what would be his weapon of choice? What would be his strategy?

Let's look at some of the historical backdrop of this meeting with the Philistines by David and Shammah!

In Matthew Henry's Concise Commentary

23:8-39 David once earnestly longed for the water at the well of Bethlehem. It seems to be an instance of weakness. He was thirsty; with the water of that well he had often refreshed himself when a youth, and it was without due thought that he desired it. Were his valiant men so forward to expose themselves, upon the least hint of their prince's mind, and so eager to please him, and shall not we long to approve ourselves to our Lord Jesus, by ready compliance with his will, as shown us by his word, Spirit, and providence? But David poured out the water as a drink-offering to the Lord. Thus he would cross his own foolish fancy, and punish himself for indulging it, and show that he had sober thoughts to correct his rash ones, and knew how to deny himself. Did David look upon that water as very precious which was got at the hazard of these men's blood, and shall not we much more value those benefits for purchasing which our blessed Saviour shed his blood?

Let all beware of neglecting so great salvation.

These soldiers had been trained by David in the arts of exercises of war, and set them an example of conduct and courage. It is the reputation as well as the advantage of a prince to be attended and served by such brave men as are here described.

For the honour of those worthies themselves, who were instrumental to bring David to the crown, settle and protect him in the throne, and enlarge his conquests. Note, those that in public stations venture themselves, and lay out themselves, to serve the interests of their country, are worthy of double honour, both to be respected by those of their own age and to be remembered by posterity.

To excite those that come after to a generous emulation. To show how much religion contributes to the inspiring of men with true courage.

David, both by his psalms and by his offerings for the service of the temple, greatly promoted piety among the grandees of the kingdom.

In I Chronicles 29:6, when they became famous for piety, they became famous for bravery. Now these mighty men are here divided into three ranks:

1. The first three, who had done the greatest exploits and thereby gained the greatest reputation-

- o Adino (v. 8),
- o Eleazar (v. 9, 10), and
- o Shammah, v. 11, 12.

I do not remember that we read of any of these, or of their actions, any where in all the story of David but here and in the parallel place, of I Chronicles 11 where many great and remarkable events are passed by in the annals, which relate rather the blemishes than the glories of David's reign, especially after his sin in the matter Uriah; so that we may conclude his reign to have been really more illustrious than it has appeared to us while reading the records of it. The exploits of this brave triumvirate are here recorded.

They signalized themselves in the wars of Israel against their enemies, especially the Philistines.

1. Adino slew 800 at once with his spear.
2. Eleazar defied the Philistines, as they by Goliath, had defied Israel, but with better success and greater bravery; for when the men of Israel had gone away, he not only kept his ground, but arose, and smote the Philistines, on whom God struck a terror equal to the courage with which this great hero was inspired. His hand was weary, and yet it clave to his sword; as long as he had any strength remaining he held his weapon and followed his blow. Thus, in the service of God, we should keep up the willingness and resolution of the spirit, notwithstanding the weakness and weariness of the flesh-faint, yet pursuing in

Judges 8:4, the hand weary, yet not quitting the sword. Now that Eleazar had beaten the enemy, the men of Israel, who had gone away from the battle

In verse 9 they returned to spoil

In verse 10 it was common for those who quit the field, when any thing is to be done to hasten to it when any thing is to be gotten. The next soldier of distinction -

3. Shammah met with a party of the enemy, that were foraging, and routed them in vs 11 and 12. But observe, both concerning this exploit and the former, it is here said, The Lord wrought a great victory. Note, How great soever the bravery of the instruments is, the praise of the achievement must be given to God. These fought the battles, but God wrought the victory. Let not the strong man then glory in his strength, nor in any of his military operations, but let him that glories glory in the Lord.

The next three were distinguished from, and dignified above, the thirty, but attained not to the first three, v. 23.

<u>All great men are not of the same size.</u>

Many a bright and benign star there is which is not of the first magnitude, and many a good ship not of the first rate.

CHAPTER 6

Location Location Location

6- Location, Location, Location

In the Cave of Adullam, meaning justice of the people, we find the anointed King David, but even though he had been anointed by the Prophet Samuel under the directions of God. He had not yet reached his set and appointed time or place. We see him in hiding and isolation and being tended to by the people in that region. People who were business merchants from the town of Canaan. David represented a people that represented justice in the eyes of God. Saul represented injustice in the way he dealt with David.

When the enemy uses a person it is with the persons own will that has allowed entry into his spirit. We see Sauls' spirit under the control of Satan and it is his intent to destroy David and not think of the consequences to the people or its land. We see the prophetic call of Jesus by Isaiah that the government would be upon his shoulders, here in the cave of Adullam a place of justice of the people, government was being forged and wealth being accrued to build the temple by his son Solomon.

Out of this city of merchants soldiers are arising, and not all of the same size in skill!

This second group of soldiers who rise to prominence there are two named

Abishai and Benaiah

Those aforementioned and these two each attended David in his troubles and suffered with him while he was hiding in isolation carrying the anointing of King on his head!

We again see the prophecy of Jesus being shown in Davids isolation, that if we would reign with him we must also suffer with him.

When David and his brave men who attended him, who had acted so vigorously against the Philistines, were, by the iniquity of the times, in Saul's reign, driven to shelter themselves from his rage in caves and strong holds, no marvel that the Philistines pitched in the valley of Rephaim, and put a garrison even in Bethlehem itself, in verse 13 and 14.

If the church's guides are so misled as to

persecute some of her best friends and champions, the common enemy will, no doubt, get advantage by it.

If David had had his liberty, Bethlehem would not have been now in the Philistines' hands. But, being so, we are here told how earnestly David longed for the water of the well of Bethlehem. Some make it a public-spirited wish, and that he meant, "O that we could drive the garrison of the Philistines out of Bethlehem, and make that beloved city of mine our own again!" the well being put for the city, as the river often signifies the country it passes through. But if he meant so, those about him did not understand him; therefore it seems rather to be an instance of his weakness. It was harvest-time; the weather was hot; he was thirsty; perhaps good water was scarce, and therefore he earnestly wished, "O that I could but have one draught of the water of the well of Bethlehem!" With the water of that well he had often refreshed himself when he was a youth, and nothing now will serve him but that, though it is almost impossible to come at it. He strangely indulged a humour which he could give no reason for. Other water might quench his thirst as well, but he had a fancy for that above any. It is folly to entertain such fancies and greater folly to insist upon the gratification of them. We ought to check our appetites when they go out inordinately towards those things that really are more pleasant and grateful than other things (Be not desirous of dainties), much more when they are thus set upon such things as only please a humour. How bravely his three mighty men, Abishai, Benaiah, and another not named, ventured through the camp of the Philistines, upon the very mouth of danger, and fetched water from the well of Bethlehem, without David's knowledge.

In verse 16, When he wished for it he was far from desiring that any of his men should venture their lives for it; but those three did, to show, First, How much they valued their prince, and with what pleasure they could run the greatest hardships in his service.

David, though anointed king, was as yet an exile, a poor prince that had no external advantages to recommend him to the affection and esteem of his attendants, nor was he in any capacity to prefer or reward them; yet those three were thus zealous for his satisfaction, firmly believing the time of recompence would come.

Let us be willing to venture in the cause of Christ, even when it is a suffering cause, as those who are assured that it will prevail and that we shall not lose by it at last. Were they so forward to expose themselves upon the least hint of their prince's mind and so ambitious to please him?

And shall not we covet to approve ourselves to our Lord Jesus by a ready compliance with every intimation of his will given us by his word, Spirit and providence?

Secondly, How little they feared the Philistines. They were glad of an occasion to defy them. Whether they broke through the host clandestinely, and with such art that the Philistines did not discover them, or openly, and with such terror in their looks that the Philistines durst not oppose them, is not certain; it should seem, they forced their way, sword in hand.

How self-denyingly David, when he had this far-fetched dear-bought water, poured it out before the Lord, verse 17. First, Thus he would show the tender regard he had to the lives of his soldiers, and how far he was from being prodigal of their blood, Ps. 72:14. In God's sight the death of his saints is precious.

Secondly, thus he would testify his sorrow for speaking that foolish word which occasioned those men to put their lives in their hands. Great men should take heed what they say, lest any bad use be made of it by those about them.

Thirdly, thus he would prevent the like rashness in any of his men for the future.

Fourthly, thus he would cross his own foolish fancy, and punish himself for entertaining and indulging it, and show that he had sober thoughts to correct his rash ones, and knew how to deny himself even in that which he was most fond of. Such generous mortifications become the wise, the great, and the good.

Fifthly, thus he would honour God and give glory to him. The water purchased at this rate he thought too precious for his own drinking and fit only to be poured out to God as a drink-offering. If it was the blood of these men, it was God's due, for the blood was always his.

Sixthly,…speaks of some who think that David hereby showed that it was not material water he longed for, but the Messiah, who had the water of life, who, he knew, should be born at Bethlehem, which the Philistines therefore should not be able to destroy.

Seventhly, did David look upon that water as very precious which was got at the hazard of these men's blood, and shall not we much more value those benefits for the purchasing of which our blessed Saviour shed his blood?

Let us not undervalue the blood of the covenant, as those do that undervalue the blessings of the covenant.

The brave actions of two of them on other occasions. Abishai slew 300 men at once, in verses 18 and 19. Benaiah did many great things. He slew two Moabites that were lion-like men, so bold and strong, so fierce and furious. He slew an Egyptian, on what occasion it is not said; he was well armed but Benaiah attacked him with no other weapon than a walking staff, dexterously wrested his spear out of his hand, and slew him with it, verse. 21. For these and similar exploits David preferred him to be captain of the life-guard or standing forces, verse 23. Inferior to the second three, but of great note, were the thirty-one here mentioned by name, verse 24, etc. Asahel is the first, who was slain by Abner in the beginning of David's reign, but lost not his place in this catalogue. Elhanan is the next, brother to Eleazar, one of the first three, verse 9.

CHAPTER 7

Let us Esteem One Another

7- Let Us Esteem One Another

Hebrews 12:15, 22 and 27.

"Looking diligently lest any man fall of the grace of God; lest any root of bitterness springing up trouble you, and thereby many be defiled…But ye are come unto mount Zion, and unto the city of the living God, the heavenly Jerusalem, and to an innumerable company of angels…And this word, Yet once more, signifieth the removing of those things that are shaken, as of things that are made, that those things which cannot be shaken may remain."

and James 1:17 through 21

"Every good gift and every perfect gift is from above, and cometh down from the Father of lights, with whom is no variableness, neither shadow or turning. Of his own will begat he us with the word of truth, that we should be a kind of firstfruits of his creatures..Wherefore my beloved brethren, let every man be swift to hear, slow to speak, slow to wrath: For the wrath of man worketh not the righteousness of God. Wherefore lay apart all filthiness and superfluity of naughtiness, and receive with meekness the engrafted word, which is able to save your souls."

"In Genesis Chapter 3, Adam and Eve became imperfect. Full of darkness and the absence of light and Adam for the first time in his life saw himself as a failure!

Eve loses direct communication with God as an equal to Adam. Both of their desires change toward God and each other. Eve loses her place of refuge in Adam as his closest advisor, so they begin to say you just don't understand me. Deception was born into the heart of mankind through the seed Satan planted in them! Since the time of the fall a wide door throughout the ages has been opened to divide relationships on every level through the deeds of deception! Instead of selflessness we now have self-centeredness. All of this occurred and more because of what happened in Genesis 3:2-6. They touched the forbidden tree of good and evil in the midst, the center of the Garden of Eden, which was the key to abundant life. Which is also connected to the Tithe. The tree possessed the element of blessing as long as Adam and Eve were obedient, everything in the Garden focused in the center – because it represented God's commandment......Proverbs 7:1-3, says "MY SON, keep my words, and lay up my commandments with thee. Keep my commandments, and live, and my law as the apple of thine eye. Bind them upon they fingers, write them upon the table of thine heart."...

The penalty of the law was given when God told Adam and Eve to not eat of the forbidden tree, this was the seal of Government in the Garden of Eden...once the seal of the law was broken, lawlessness spread throughout the entire creation....a curse comes upon the lawless. God does not have to curse anything or anybody, simply violate the law that is governing that part of the universe and you reap the curse. I have set before you life and death, blessings and cursing – choose life, God said. Malachi 3:6-13,18 references the blessing and the cursing. The center of man's existence is dependent on his desires towards God…

Adam robbed God, cursed his seed and his house, and birthed the spirit of conflict into the world's system (Satan's domain, Genesis 3:3).

Within our desires towards God lies a struggle of selfishness versus self-sacrifice.

Before the fall we were fixed on communion with our CREATOR! Since the fall we have dimmed the lights on the line of communication. It has been said that our eyes are the window to our souls.

Windows serve a two-fold purpose, to see others and to be seen. God looks through the window of our eyes to see into our souls! What does he see when he looks through your windows Selah - pause and think about it!

Shadow

Have you ever seen a lamp that is lit and a sheer cover with a tint of color in it lay over the lamp thus creating an ambience of softness to the room It changes the brightness of the light and the mood of the room changes, so it is with mankind - our mood and/or countenance changes when the shadows of the works of the flesh are displayed. It is like a shadow that passes in front of you and blocks out the light and the environment is charged with the presence of darkness.

This is in essence the shadow that comes up before the candle of God (the Holy Spirit) inside of a Christian. There is a change in the color of a person and the brightness of their countenance when shadow(s) exist within them. This signifies that duplicity in nature is at war with the spirit of God. It is the spirit of God that wills to do good in and through us. When we refuse to walk in the divine nature of God and walk after the flesh a shadowing occurs that is visibly discernable by the

Holy Spirit. For this reason we must know those that labor among us. Be not deceived God is not mocked whatever a man soweth that shall he also reap! Deception is rampant in the world! Even in the Body of Christ! The Bible records that if it be possible even the very elect will be deceived. Discernment! Discernment! Discernment!

Discernment come forth in the sons of God for such a time in the Kingdom of God, in Jesus Name. Amen! We must be like the sons of Issachar during this hour!

Deception

The ability to take a measure of truth and cloak it in a series of lies.

When we are no longer deceived by ulterior motives and selfish ambition, but fully intent on doing only the will of the Master. We are vessels of honor fit to be used in the Kingdom of God, as long as your kingdom exist there is the presence of the root of deception that produces Shadows and Turning!

Hebrews 12:15, 22 and 27.

"Looking diligently lest any man fall of the grace of God; lest any root of bitterness springing up trouble you, and thereby many be defiled...But ye are come unto mount Zion, and unto the city of the living God, the heavenly Jerusalem, and to an innumerable company of angels...And this word, Yet once more, signifieth the removing of those things that are shaken, as of things that are made, that those things which cannot be shaken may remain."

... and James 1:17 through 21

Armour of Light

Romans 13:11-14 says to us twelve commands of how we are to conduct ourselves before God! "And that, knowing the time, that now it is high time to awake out of sleep: for now is our salvation nearer than when we believed.

The night is far spent, the day is at hand: let us therefore cast off the works of darkness, and let us put on the armour of light. (bold mine) Let us walk honestly, as in the day not in rioting and drunkenness, Not in chambering, and wantonnness (quarreling), not in strife and envying (jealousies) But put ye on the Lord Jesus Christ, and make not provision for the flesh, to fulfill the lusts thereof. Somebody has to rule and somebody has to reign and somebody has to serve!

Abdication

Many of us have abdicated the throne room in exchange for the pig pen. We have relinquished and surrendered our royal ring, robe, crest and power for things we were never predestined to have. Because of this we find ourselves wandering like vagabonds with no permanent home or place of sanctuary!

The worst choice any human can make is to live his life without God on board! Detours cause delays, but thanks be unto God they don't have to become denials! Gifts and callings are without repentance!

And we have a high priest who is making intercession for us! But how long shall we stand halted between two opinions! If God be God then serve God! Choose you this day whom you will serve!

If you are detoured and delayed, I pray you will get back on track so your delay does not become a denial. Remember many will call upon the name of the Lord, and he will ask who they are and politely tell them I know you not! Is your name about to be blotted out where it matters most!

You can be on the guest list of Governors, Presidents, CEO and Charities and miss being on the family roll call of Heaven! Exchange ownership of your life through submission to the rightful owner, who is none other than Your Creator - God!

Submission

Is not slavery or bondage, but recognition of the spirit of God within us as our authority or owner! Submitting to God first means we commit totally to his directives and his authority over us! When someone who has authority meets another who is in authority they will acquiesce to the one who has the most authority by locale and region. They are not submitting to the person who holds the office but the office aka position that person occupies. When we encounter God it should be obvious who has the authority in that meeting place! We know that all authority has been given by God and he allows one man to be put up and another put down, because God has ordained the office and this is what we submit to. Such offices as Parent, Husband, Wife, Pastor and Governing officials are offices ordained by God! It does not require your liking the person occupying the office but loving the God who ordained the office! The office is the vehicle of their authority and getting their job completed is all that is of any consequence while holding that office! When we view submission this way it no longer becomes male or female, Black or White, Likes You or Doesn't Like You! We surrender to Gods' will so that it may go well with us according to the blessings of Deuteronomy.

Surrender

Give up your rights to control your world to God! We own nothing that will be taken with us on the eternal exit. It all belongs to God and he is lending us the vessel (our bodies) its' contents and all the accumulated wealth temporarily for His good pleasure! The earth is the Lord's and the fullness thereof!

We are stewards as the Bible speaks of the vineyard and the vine dressers stating that each is worthy of their hire, no matter what time they started to work! The wage is set, seems unjust! It is not like you reported to work late in the day and received pay, but you reported as soon as you were hired to do the work measured out to you and for that you were offered a wage equal to one who had started earlier. Grace is in operation in the passage of the laborers in the vineyard, because many are falling away and the last shall be first! We like the idea of possessing and owning, and all we are doing is putting to the exchange what belongs to God!

When we make a quality decision to let go and do it God's way always! We must acknowledge that God knows whats best and the final outcome is known by him! Doesn't mean we agree 100% but we acknowledge that he knows better than we do and we are mere specks of dust, with at best a three pound brain attempting to dictate to the mind of God who is the brain creator! We must become his and allow him to become ours! He said that he would be our God and we would be his people! Through reconciliation and the spirit of adoption we are endued with power. Givien joint authority; heirship to reign, to rule and to rest in the Kingdom of God through the Death, Burial, Resurrection and Ascension of Jesus Christ!

Death

We have died to ourselve and no longer behaving as a dictator telling the brain maker how to run our lives. We no longer have to pay the penalty of sin;

which was eternal death, because we had a substitute stand in for us on our day of reckoning! The death penalty was not thrown out but completed through Jesus Christ! We are not dying as Jesus died a physical death that was the penalty for sin! He obeyed in our place completely so we would only have to die a spiritual death through receiving the gift of salvation purchased by his death on the cross! We submit our flesh to the power of the Holy Spirit to reign over our flesh in dominion by the authority of the Holy Spirit to Gods' will! Which is the Word of God! We become clothed in righteousness when we pass through death through submission, exchanging your will for God will because it is our reasonable service! After all we were released from the debtors prison!

Burial

Placing your will under the blood of Jesus and relinquishing the existence of self-willed living in exchange for a surrendered way of living. Everything about us is placed in the soil of the

Word of God. We die inside of that soil as seed dies under the crushing power of the death packed upon it! The shell it crushed, the outer man as the Word of God says must die daily! Until the blade of the new life is able to overcome the hard outer shell and push its way up through the dirt that was once its grave! When it springs out from beneath the dirt it has gained authority over that dirt! My God! Oh grave where is your victory and death where is your sting. He got up from the dirt that was stacked on him for us and it can no longer hold us down! Can you imagine going to the cemetery and laying down next to an occupied grave to tell the grave attendant to pour dirt on you because you are dead. Clearly dead men don't talk to the grave attendants! How foolish that would be for the attendant to say, okay and begin pouring dirt on top of you as you lay on top of the ground! Because it would be illegal for him to dig a hole and bury you alive; he would be guilty of murder! This is what we are doing when we lay down and act as if we have no hope; surely –

surely! Get up from there, no matter what you have been through you cannot legally occupy a grave anymore until it is your time! You can hasten the day of your reburial, but look there is really no reason to die an eternal death through suicide. When you have the right to eternal life! You are miserable here on earth you believe, from what the Bible says you will be really miserable spending eternity in hell! Allow the Word of God to wash, transform, renew your way of thinking by accepting him not just as your Savior, but also as your Lord. You can be saved and not allow Jesus to be the Lord of your life. Have your ticket punched to get on board and everything and just take a your position when he comes back and just be glad you are going to heaven! Or you can stay right here and bring heaven down to this earthly existence you dread so much! Paul teaches us how to abase and abound, and with whatever time you have left down here you should want to really cause Satan and his imps some discomfiting! He hates our praise and worship of God! He hates for us to realize that God is greater than anything we are going through and in turn magnify him above the circumstances! He hates the fact that you get to live where he can never live again! He hates us when we become the Sons of God, because he knows what we are entitled to as Sons! Satan is a liar, a deceiver and destroyer of all that God has meant for good in your life! He comes to steal, kill and destroy and he is 100% committed to his purpose, and that is to keep you from being 100% committed to your purpose! Come on get up and wash your face, hands and feet! Anoint yourself and put on the Lord Jesus Christ! We are the Sons of the Most High God by Position and not Gender! He makes us hate who we are and leads us into self-mutilation of our bodies as a way of hurting God! How can the clay say to the potter why have you made me like this! He made you for his good pleasure in His image! If something genetically has affected your life don't blame it on God, Satan is the one who seeks to pervert all that God creates. God is not a dictator, and sometimes defects occur due to various reasons that exist in the earth, but the original plan of man was not flawed! Because God said everything he made was good and very good! When Adam saw his rib manifest in front of his eyes beyond his wildest expectation he did not identify with himself or a clone of himself but a part of himself that would enable him to fulfill purpose; be fruitful and multiply, subdue and have dominion as God instructed!

Resurrection

The seed of salvation is crushed and the blade comes forth and springs forth into a new life. It sheds the hard shell that confined the mystery of life and causes us to spring forth united to God as heirs and joint heirs of his only begotten son so that we may take not just any seat, but our rightful seat, wear our righteous attire; no more fig leaves and to be in our righteous minds – let this mind be in you which was in Christ Jesus!

Being about his Fathers Business   Ruling, Reigning, Subduing and Multiplying in Purpose!

Ascension

We are seated with Jesus Christ as joint heirs in heavenly places because when he ascended we were granted access to ascend too, after he poured out his spirit on all flesh in Acts. Jesus sealed the redemption of man forever in heaven and transferred us from the penalty of death into the promise of everlasting life and that being the Zoe life – the God life we were intended to have. Jesus sealed the redemption. Jesus said Father prepare me a body and I will redeem man back to you! Here we are now empowered to be sons and daughters of obedience and recipients of covenant promises! Engrafted into the family of the Abrahamic Covenant

Covenant

This covenant was written in the flesh of Jesus through his many wounds, stripes and crown of thorns. Seventy-two (72) crowns for the nations pierced his head and thirty-nine (39) stripes bore on his body for the diseases of man, and five (5) wounds in his flesh to move us out of the dispensation of the law and into grace! He has made a way of escape from every temptation, trial and test and the directions to the pathway is written in the precious, powerful and pure blood of the paschal lamb! He has placed His name on us and given us the Ring of Sonship and clothed us in the Robe of His Beloved!

Ring Giver

He placed on our finger a ring symbolizing reconciliation as the Father did with the prodigal son and declared us no longer bastards and wayward. We are positionally Sons of the most High God! He further consummates the marriage of the Bridegroom by placing a ring inside of us that says we are his beloved, sealed in our spiritual hearts. Because he consummates with Spirit and not with Flesh as he did with Mary! He carried us into the Bridal chamber by accepting our intimacy offering and we have become one with him! Through spiritual sanctification, renewal came into my life and He released me from the defilement of the impurities in my soul! He shared with me that for every person I had been intimate with, whether willingingly or unwillingly a ring was placed inside of me! When he says that the two become one he was literally meaning that a ring is hidden inside of the uterus. It is clear to see where man is the Ring Maker in the earthly from by the shape of the circular tip of a man's penis. When he enters a womb he marks a woman internally in her secret parts as belonging to another that is not visible to the human eye! But for his good pleasure we are sealed! A covered well that cannot be defiled, a garden enclosed for private ownership!

God gave me the phrase "Ring Maker" during this journey and there is a process that he has shared with me during this journey that has restored him as the rightful Ring Maker in my life at this present writing! When a husband marries his wife he places his ring, his signet, his authority inside of her and she is fitted to be his until death does them part! During this journey God confirmed this revelation to me about "The Ring Maker" while viewing a true forensics documentary, where the uterus of cadabres that had been prostitutes were studied! The scientist illustrated how the inside lining of the wall of the uterus had varying circles; he explained these were obviously marks from the varying sexual relations a woman has had over her lifetime! God is awesome and his omniscience covers all things men and women of God!! He intended us for his good pleasure on every level Spiritually to be exclusive with him and not unfaithful as Gomer was to Hosea! He has place a ring on a natural man to act as a seal of authority in the womb of his woman. Much like the wearer of a Royal Signet Ring would stamp his seal of authority in wax when sealing an envelope or document! God gave man the ring he needed to crown his wife with physically as the "Ring Giver" as he had spiritually been the "Ring Giver" and empowered man to be the physical "Ring Maker" and God to be the spiritual ring maker, as two become one in the spirit; and in the flesh! Whose wife are you ladies? Whose husband are you gentlemen! We perish for a lack of knowledge; to have been taught like this we would have treated ourselves with much greater respect on all accounts! God Be Praised! SELAH!

Ring Maker

God is the maker of all things! He made the World, so that he could sit on the circle of the earth! He made the Galaxies and Solar Systems, and the concept of circular motion. He exist and we exist because we live and move and have our being in him. Every life bearing creation from God exist in a circle. The stem of a flower is circular (tubular), the trees are circular and the males penis is circular, and the womans vaginal opening is circular. This circular notion is perpetuated through the Life Cycle of Man and the Universe. God placed a ring embosser on the tip of a mans' penis that would create an imprint in the wall of a womans uterine lining that would mark her as his in the hidden parts. Selah!

Women think on this – how many men have placed a ring inside of you! Stop and think about this, could this be why so many marriages are in trouble. Because of the hauntings and clanging of rings inside that remind us of the way it use to be! Men think on this – how many women have you left your ring inside of, luring you to come back for seconds for old times sake! Your visual memory bank rolls out that footage more than you care to admit! (Smile) God has it all under consideration children. We are suffering in our hearts; some consciously and some unconsciously because of the hidden rings that lay inside of us where we have collected inside of us as women and men have deposited! Sometimes we are given different rings by suitors and we keep them and wear them on every finger if necessary! Can you think with me for a moment that your outward display is a mirror to what is going on inside of your uterus. You keep the rings because you feel entitled to keep them and display them, and you cannot get pass the memories of the rings inside of you! Could there be a connection? Just a thought? Ask God about it! Can you envision those rings stacked up on your fingers are stacked up inside of you while you are intimately involved with the next person. They can't reach your heart because of the traffic jam inside, and men you can't give your heart for remembering all of the rings you gave away and who you gave them to and why you gave them away! So she can't get into your heart because there is no room to receive her gift inside of your heart! Old haunted houses!

Ring Wearer

How many rings are you still wearing my Sister, and how many ring receipts are you carrying in your pocket my Brother? The wearer of a ring given upon betrothal, proposal or marriage is in covenant "Hased" just as God is in covenant with us! He has placed a ring of reconciliation upon our right hand and received us into the fellowship of his dear children and saints of God! We are never to take lightly the covenant we carry in our hearts because of the fulfillment of the plan of salvation. Many of us wear multiple rings on both hands for decorative reasons. When we wear a ring on the left wedding finger it is forever a ring that we enter into with the intent to stay in covenant forever. Think about it when that ring is placed on your finger you slide into it with tenderness and reverence and adoration for the one who is placing it on your finger. You are so desirous of making this last forever! The ring that you receive at salvation is forever, unless you take the ring off and turn back to your old ways!

Yet, God declares in Revelations that he is married to the backslider – he never never divorces us! How many newly engaged women do you see walking around with a sad demeanor, or glum look on their faces! I have never seen one! Even when a man is engaged he has a certain look about him and a look in his eyes when he sees her walk in the room! When we receive Christ into our hearts it is him placing his imprint in our inward man, and we are so full of excitement and we want to run and tell everybody about this experience we had! Just like the woman at the well in Samaria! I recall what the old saints would say, it gets sweeter and sweeter as the days go by! Never understood that until I came to know him fully for myself, and now I too consider it getting sweeter and sweeter as the days go by! I hope that I even look more like him! When married couples have been together for awhile they start to resemble each other, don't they Well, we should as the ring wearer of salvation look more like the ring giver too! We could take this much deeper, but the intent here is to steer you into the marriage supper, because the bride groom cometh! Will you be ready Don't be left out like the five foolish virgins without any oil in their lamp! It is time for you and I too manifest as the Sons and Daughters of the Most High God!

Reign

He has elevated us to a new position of righteousness and spread a robe on us and called us royalty (worthy) to be in his presence. Endued with certain rights and authority to reign and have dominion as he originally intended! Have you seen a reigning King or Queen who always stands up, reigning requires we take our rightful seats! We have been made heirs and joint-heirs through Christ Jesus! We are seated in heavenly places. You can stand and rule, but you can not stand and reign! Reigning rulers occupy seats assigned for them for the duration and a ruler must come to rest in that office by being seated and receiving the benefits of reigning his kingdom! He daily loads us with benefits! We are the ones who wander the wilderness like vagabonds because we are still living on Manna and not feasting at the Kings Table! The Table has been set now for awhile for us!

The surnames here given them are taken, as it should seem, from the places of their birth or habitation, as many surnames with us originally were. From all parts of the nation, the most wise and valiant were picked up to serve the king. Several of those who are named we find captains of the twelve courses which David appointed, one for each month in the year, I Chronicles 27.

Those that did worthily were preferred according to their merits. One of them was the son of Ahithophel (verse 34), the son famous in the camp as the father at the council-board. But to find Uriah the Hittite bringing up the rear of these worthies, as it revives the remembrance of David's sin, so it aggravates it, that a man who deserved so well of his king and country should be so ill treated.

Joab is not mentioned among all these, either, to be mentioned; the first, of the first three sat chief among the captains, but Joab was over them as general.

Because he was so bad that he did not deserve to be mentioned; for though he was confessedly a great soldier, and one that had so much religion in him as to dedicate of his spoils to the house of God (I Chronicles 26:28), yet he lost as much honour by slaying two of David's friends as ever he got by slaying his enemies.

Christ, the Son of David, has his worthies too, who like David's, are influenced by his example, fight his battles against the spiritual enemies of his kingdom, and in his strength are more than conquerors.

Christ's apostles were his immediate attendants, did and suffered great things for him, and at length came to reign with him. They are mentioned with honour in the New Testament, as these in the Old, especially, Revelation 21:14.

Nay, all the good soldiers of Jesus Christ have their names better preserved than even these worthies have; for they are written in heaven.

    This honour have all his saints and in the practical art of war, the best thing of all is to take the enemy's country whole and intact rather than to destroy it in the natural, but oftentimes God will require that an entire country be destroyed as with the Agagites of which Haman was a descendant. God told Saul through the Prophet Samuel to not leave anything alive nor spare any animal or take any spoils from that land. Those orders were not carried out and years later God raises up a handmaiden through Esther for such a time that would come when the consequences of their disobedience would face them through the hand of Haman seeking the total destruction of the Jews. This is why it is important to seek the Lord about who you are to entertain and who you are to join ranks with and the logistics of the battle! We are not to walk in our own wisdom or our own desires! To fight all the time is not always the plan of God. What does God say is always the best choice to take when you are uncertain about the strategy and the means by which God will accomplish the Word of God over your life!

Jesus made of himself no reputation, yet he perfectly defeated the enemy by making no mistakes of disobedience!

What the ancients called a clever fighter is one who not only wins, but excels in winning with ease. Hence his victories bring him neither reputation for wisdom nor credit for courage. He wins his battles by making no mistakes that will cost them more than they can afford!

Making no mistakes of disobedience and should you be quick to get it corrected is what establishes the certainty of victory, for it means conquering an enemy that is already defeated.

CHAPTER 8

The Devil Is a Liar

8- The Devil is a Liar

Making no mistakes of disobedience and should you be quick to get it corrected is what establishes the certainty of victory, for it means conquering an enemy that is already defeated.

...Thy pomp is brought down to the grave, and the noise of thy viols, the worm is spread under thee, and the worms cover thee. How art thou fallen from heaven, O Lucifer, son of the morning! how art thou cut down to the ground, which didst weaken the nations!

Why! Because thou hast said in thine heart...

- I will ascend into heaven,
- I will exalt my throne above the stars (the angels) of God:
- I will sit also upon the mount of the congregation, in the sides of the north;
- I will ascend above the heights of the clouds:
- I will be like the most High (take God's place).

Yet thou shalt be brought down to hell, to the sides of the pit. They that see thee shall be brought down to hell, to the sides of the pit."(Christians) have focused on what Satan is doing and not on what Satan can not do! We give him credit where there is no credit due him, where things are out of order in our lives, we need look no further than the mirror! I am speaking of free will choices, not choices that were made or forced on us!

Don't get angry, get free of the bondage that you have created by being led away by your own desires and lust! James 1:14 –15 says "But each one is tempted when he is drawn away by his own desires and enticed. Then, when desire has conceived, it gives birth to sin; and sin, when it is full-grown, brings forth death."

The number nine (9) is the number of the Holy Spirit, of completeness, finality, and fulness. There are 9 Gifts and most have been taught that there are nine (9) Fruits; including myself. After further study and understanding that there is only one (1) fruit with a nine-fold expression. Much like you would see an orange or a pomegranate has sections, but is only one fruit! Which further explains the presence of pomegranates between each bell on the hem of the High Priest garments.

We have one seed sown in the womb of a woman and 9 months for the expression to manifest outwardly! Even in twin births they begin as one then splits!

Satan tries to woo us into captivity as evidenced in Jeremiah 29:30, 31; and to accomplish this Satan appeals to the soulish desires of man, his self-centered motives and aspirations for control. He appeals to mans' fallen nature of this will for self-preservation, self-fulfillment and boisterous self-grandisement.

Satan and his minions lie in wait for our souls at the gate of every door available to us to trick and manipulate us into contaminating our temples! Spiritual contamination of polluting the Body of Christ that is you, because you are the church also known as the Body. God is coming back for an overcoming church, those whose robes have been washed in the blood of the lamb!

Yet, God speaks to the heart of mans' issues and self-afflictions to teach us how to use our own dominion and power; also known as authority.

Clearly in Proverbs 6:16-19, it states that "These six things doth the Lord hate: yea, seven are an abomination unto him that are a part of Satan's arsenal.

We have had the choices of others imposed on us and we have made our choices based on those choices. Now it is time to grow in the wisdom of God and undo some of those choices that were detrimental!

God Hates -

A Proud Look Uplifted eyes and high-minded actions that perceives oneself as greater than the rest of their associates or humankind.

A Lying Tongue hates the truth and has no desire to speak the truth.

Hands that Shed Innocent Blood are hands that waste the blood of others who have not committed injustices against them or others are guilty of murder or brutalities.

A Heart that Deviseth Wicked Imaginations is a heart that plots the down-fall of others by lying, planting and building evil and malicious thoughts in their minds and others that create scandals and destruction.

Feet that be Swift in Running to Mischief have you ever seen people that will run to the scene of a fight or crime quickly trying to be the first to witness what is happening and quickly observe the scene and begin sensationalizing the details. They can hardly wait to go tell their version of what happened regardless to having missed the beginning of the turn of events.

A False Witness that Speaketh Lies and this one is self-explanatory because they are incapable of speaking of the truth even under oath.

He that Soweth Discord (Abomination) "To his soul." They trouble – trouble! Because they are so full of mischief and vain imaginations that peace escapes them. Wherever they are or go disruptions occur leaving behind stress and chaos among people.

Destroying families, friends, associates, churches, and anyone who eats their lies and misrepresentations. Wickedness that binds and twist the mind by wicked thoughts and actions towards brethren like wicker "twisted".

What About Satan

"Isaiah 14:4,9,10-15 "That thou shalt take up this proverb against the king of Babylon, and say, How hath the oppressor ceased! The golden city ceased!...Hell from beneath is moved for thee to meet thee at thy coming: it stirreth up the dead for thee, even all the chief ones of the earth; it hath raised up from their thrones all the kings of the nations. All they shall speak and say unto thee, Art thou also become weak as we art thou become like unto us Thy pomp is brought down to the grave, and the noise of thy viols, the worm is spread under thee, and the worms cover thee. How art thou fallen from heaven, O Lucifer, son of the morning! how art thou cut down to the ground, which didst weaken the nations!

Why! Because thou hast said in thine heart…

- I will ascend into heaven,
- I will exalt my throne above the stars (the angels) of God:
- I will sit also upon the mount of the congregation, in the sides of the north;
- I will ascend above the heights of the clouds:
- I will be like the most High (take God's place).

Yet thou shalt be brought down to hell, to the sides of the pit. They that see thee shall be brought down to hell, to the sides of the pit."…(Christians) have focused on what Satan is doing and not on what Satan can not do! We give him credit where there is no credit due him, where things are out of order in our lives, we need look no further than the mirror! I am speaking of free will choices, not choices that were made or forced on us!

The one who gives power to all of us, gave him his power and devices to him. The power given to Satan by God is real, but not greater than the power God has given his people. We even falsely accuse Satan of being at the root of our failures. Don't get angry, get free of the bondage that you have created by being led away by your own desires and lust!

James 1:14 –15 says "But each one is tempted when he is drawn away by his own desires and enticed. Then, when desire has conceived, it gives birth to sin; and sin, when it is full-grown, brings forth death." The bottom line is that Satan's destiny is defined in Ezekiel 28:12-19 and Revelation 12:7,10,12. Ezekiel 28:12-19(NKJV) reads "Son of man, take up your lamentation for the king of Tyre, and say to him, 'Thus says the Lord God:

"You were the seal of perfection, Full of wisdom and perfect in beauty…You were in Eden, the garden of God; Every precious stone was your covering:

The sardius, topaz, and diamond, beryl, onyx, and jasper, sapphire, turquoise, and emerald with gold. The workmanship of your timbrels and pipes was prepared for you on the day you were created. "You were the anointed cherub who covers; I established you; you were on the holy mountain of God; …You walked back and forth in the midst of the fiery stones. You were perfect in your ways from the day you were created. Till iniquity was found in you. By the abundance of your trading You became filled with violence within, And you sinned; …Therefore I cast you as a profane thing Out of the mountain of God; And I destroyed you, O covering cherub, From the midst of the fiery stones. Your heart was lifted up because of your beauty; You corrupted your wisdom for the sake of your splendor; I cast you to the ground, I laid you before kings, That they might gaze at you. You defiled your sanctuaries by the multitude of your iniquities, By the iniquity of your trading; Therefore I brought fire from your midst; It devoured you, And I turned you to ashes upon the earth In the sight of all who saw you. All who knew you among the peoples are astonished at you; You have become a horror, And shall be no more forever." Lucifer received from God at the moment of his creation: a name that meant shining one, Seal of Perfection, full of Wisdom, perfect in Beauty, covered in Nine Stones and Gold. Again we see the number five (5) a symbol of God's grace.

The number nine (9) is the number of the Holy Spirit, of completeness, finality, and fulness. There are 9 Gifts, 9 Fruits, and 9 months for the "Fruit of the Womb." Timbrels (internal tambourine like drum) and Pipes (flutes or other woodwinds) with every breath he praised God, an Anointing to Cover, Established, and enabled to walk in the midst of the Fiery Stones and a Free Will.

So let's play role reversal with what Lucifer had. First his name is now Satan meaning opposer and adversary of both believer and unbeliever – nobody's friend, the seal of imperfection, full of foolishness, perfectly ugly, non-precious stones (fakes), tarnished brass, removal from the trinity and given a number assignment of six (6), representing man and not God, a beast, unfinished (suppose this is why God will finish him), and full of emptiness, instruments that condemn instead of praise, unable to praise God – can only speak curses on himself, others and to God with every breath, an anointing to uncover – point the finger (accuser of the brethren), and unable to walk in the midst of the fiery stones, but consumed by the fire.

Satan lost his free will and became subject to the children of God in the earth, and many of us don't know or act like it. Some of us are catching on, hurry, did you catch up?

I believe it is that way, and in another time and place I would love to prove it to you. For now think about it and study it for yourself!

When Adam yielded his purpose to Satan, the whole earth and all that was within the earth fell out of the divine order of God. As a result of the fall, Satan becomes god of this world (Genesis 3:11, 22-23) and Adam transferred his dominion of this world over to Satan (Genesis 3:4-5).

From that point until the Ascension of Christ, man strives for success and fulfillment that eludes him and brings fleeting pleasure (Genesis 4:3-8).

The children of man are born divided and saddled with the seed of strife and murder in their hearts (Genesis 4:9). The woman seeks to fill her void without relief with temporal things, baubles and beads. All of mankind and the earth were filled with a longing for "unity and restoration" (Genesis 4:16).

The loss of eternal life in Genesis 3:19,22 demanded a cry for a savior, and a response from a redeemer.

Satan was already on the earth dwelling in total darkness, when God came to create on the earth form and fullness. Satan had been on board left to devise weapons of assault on the earth. In an effort to stop all of mankind from returning back to communion with God in Paradise, Satan tries to woo us into captivity. (Jeremiah 29:30:, 31)

To accomplish this Satan appeals to the soulish desires of man, his self-centered motives and aspirations for control. He appeals to mans' fallen nature of the will for self-preservation, self-fulfillment and boisterous attitudes.

Ultimately his aim is to destroy God's creation by weakening the kingdom of God through wars, pestilence, hunger, plagues, homicides, murders (abortions), suicide, genocide, immorality, accusations of the Saints, and lawlessness. He uses money as the central dividing line, and the pursuit of attaining money to separate the people from one another. These are the steps and how they develop in mans' life. First, there is the love of money. Then apostasy through the unbridled desire to have the pleasures of the earth as ones' own...."

Satan and his minions lie in wait for our souls at the gate of every door available to us to trick and maninpulate us into contaminating our temples and thus polluting the Body of Christ as a whole. We are told to let the wheat and the tare grow together, and we are also told that He is coming back for an overcoming church, those whose robes have been washed in the blood of the lamb! Yet, God speaks to the heart of mans' calamities and self-afflictions and of all of them He has given us dominion and power. Clearly in Proverbs 6:16-19, it states that "These six things doth the Lord hate: yea, seven are an abomination unto him:

Jesus took the battle to the enemy and defeated him on every level so that you and I can walk in the victory he has obtained for us! In this we must find ourselves waging war in this victory where Satan is a defeated foe!

Job 4:14 Fear came upon me, and trembling, which made all my bones to shake.

Matthew Henry commentary:

Fear came upon me, "Met me." "shuddering," or "horror." Job became greatly alarmed at the vision.

Which made all my bones to shake, as in Hebrew, the multitude of my bones. A similar image is employed by Virgil, "A cold tremor ran through all their bones."

Gill's Exposition of the Entire Bible

Fear came upon me, and trembling,.... Not only a dread of mind, but trembling of body; which was often the case even with good men, whenever there was any unusual appearance of God unto them by a voice, or by any representation, or by an angel; as with Abraham in the vision of the pieces, and with Moses on Mount Sinai, and with Daniel in some of his visions, and with Zechariah, when an angel appeared and brought him the tidings of a son to be born to him; which arises from the frailty and weakness of human nature, a consciousness of guilt, a sense of the awful majesty of God, and an uneasy apprehension of what may be the consequences of it: which made all my bones to shake; not only there was inward fear and outward tremor of body, but to such a degree, that not one joint in him was still; all the members of his body shook, and every bone was as if it was loosed...

Geneva Study Bible

Fear came upon me, and trembling, which made all my bones {i} to shake.

(i) In these visions which God shows to his creatures, there is always a certain fear joined, that the authority of it might be had in greater reverence.

Matthew Henry's Concise Commentary

4:12-21 Eliphaz relates a vision. When we are communing with our own hearts, and are still, Ps 4:4, then is a time for the Holy Spirit to commune with us. This vision put him into very great fear. Ever since man sinned, it has been terrible to him to receive communications from Heaven, conscious that he can expect no good tidings thence. Sinful man! shall he pretend to be more just, more pure, than God, who being his Maker, is his Lord and Owner? How dreadful, then, the pride and presumption of man! How great the patience of God! Look upon man in his life.

The very foundation of that cottage of clay in which man dwells, is in the dust, and it will sink with its own weight. We stand but upon the dust. Some have a higher heap of dust to stand upon than others but still it is the earth that stays us up, and will shortly swallow us up. Man is soon crushed; or if some lingering distemper, which consumes like a moth, be sent to destroy him, he cannot resist it. Shall such a creature pretend to blame the appointments of God? Look upon man in his death. Life is short, and in a little time men are cut off. Beauty, strength, learning, not only cannot secure them from death, but these things die with them; nor shall their pomp, their wealth, or power, continue after them. Shall a weak, sinful, dying creature, pretend to be more just than God, and more pure than his Maker? No: instead of quarrelling with his afflictions, let him wonder that he is out of hell. Can a man be cleansed without his Maker? Will God justify sinful mortals, and clear them from guilt? or will he do so without their having an interest in the righteousness and gracious help of their promised Redeemer, when angels, once ministering spirits before his throne, receive the just recompence of their sins? Notwithstanding the seeming impunity of men for a short time, though living without God in the world, their doom is as certain as that of the fallen angels, and is continually overtaking them. Yet careless sinners note it so little, that they expect not the change, nor are wise to consider their latter end.

Matthew Henry's Whole Bible Commentary
Verses 12-21

Eliphaz, having undertaken to convince Job of the sin and folly of his discontent and impatience, here vouches a vision he had been favoured with, which he relates to Job for his conviction. What comes immediately from God all men will pay a particular deference to, and Job, no doubt, as much as any. Some think Eliphaz had this vision now lately, since he came to Job, putting words into his mouth wherewith to reason with him; and it would have been well if he had kept to the purport of this vision, which would serve for a ground on which to reprove Job for his murmuring, but not to condemn him as a hypocrite. Others think he had it formerly; for God did, in this way, often communicate his mind to the children of men in those first ages of the world, ch. 33:15. Probably God had sent Eliphaz this messenger and message some time or other, when he was himself in an unquiet discontented frame, to calm and pacify him.

Note, As we should comfort others with that wherewith we have been comforted (2 Co. 1:4), so we should endeavour to convince others with that which has been powerful to convince us. The people of God had not then any written word to quote, and therefore God sometimes notified to them even common truths by the extraordinary ways of revelation. We that have Bibles have there (thanks be to God) a more sure word to depend upon than even visions and voices, 2 Pt. 1:19.

Observe:

I. The manner in which this message was sent to Eliphaz, and the circumstances of the conveyance of it to him. 1. It was brought to him secretly, or by stealth. Some of the sweetest communion gracious souls have with God is in secret, where no eye sees but that of him who is all eye. God has ways of bringing conviction, counsel, and comfort, to his people, unobserved by the world, by private whispers, as powerfully and effectually as by the public ministry. His secret is with them, Ps. 25:14. As the evil spirit often steals good words out of the heart (Mt. 13:19), so the good Spirit sometimes steals good words into the heart, or ever we are aware. 2. He received a little thereof, v. 12. And it is but a little of divine knowledge that the best receive in this world. We know little in comparison with what is to be known, and with what we shall know when we come to heaven. How little a portion is heard of God! ch. 26:14. We know but in part, 1 Co. 13:12. See his humility and modesty. He pretends not to have understood it fully, but something of it he perceived. 3. It was brought to him in the visions of the night (v. 13), when he had retired from the world and the hurry of it, and all about him was composed and quiet. Note, The more we are withdrawn from the world and the things of it the fitter we are for communion with God. When we are communing with our own hearts, and are still (Ps. 4:4), then is a proper time for the Holy Spirit to commune with us. When others were asleep Eliphaz was ready to receive this visit from Heaven, and probably, like David, was meditating upon God in the night-watches; in the midst of those good thoughts this thing was brought to him.

We should hear more from God if we thought more of him; yet some are surprised with convictions in the night, ch. 33:14, 15. 4. It was prefaced with terrors: Fear came upon him, and trembling, v. 14. It should seem, before he either heard or saw any thing, he was seized with this trembling, which shook his bones, and perhaps the bed under him. A holy awe and reverence of God and his majesty being struck upon his spirit, he was thereby prepared for a divine visit. Whom God intends to honour he first humbles and lays low, and will have us all to serve him with holy fear, and to rejoice with trembling.

    II. The messenger by whom it was sent-a spirit, one of the good angels, who are employed not only as the ministers of God's providence, but sometimes as the ministers of his word. Concerning this apparition which Eliphaz saw we are here told (v. 15, 16), 1. That it was real, and not a dream, not a fancy. An image was before his eyes; he plainly saw it; at first it passed and repassed before his face, moved up and down, but at length it stood still to speak to him. If some have been so knavish as to impose false visions on others, and some so foolish as to be themselves imposed upon, it does not therefore follow but that there may have been apparitions of spirits, both good and bad. 2. That it was indistinct, and somewhat confused. He could not discern the form thereof, so as to frame any exact idea of it in his own mind, much less to give a description of it. His conscience was to be awakened and informed, not his curiosity gratified. We know little of spirits; we are not capable of knowing much of them, nor is it fit that we should: all in good time; we must shortly remove to the world of spirits, and shall then be better acquainted with them. 3. That it puts him into a great consternation, so that his hair stood on end. Ever since man sinned it has been terrible to him to receive an express from heaven, as conscious to himself that he can expect no good tidings thence; apparitions therefore, even of good spirits, have always made deep impressions of fear, even upon good men. How well it is for us that God sends us his messages, not by spirits, but by men like ourselves, whose terror shall not make us afraid! See Dan. 7:28; 10:8, 9.

III. The message itself. Before it was delivered there was silence, profound silence, v. 16. When we are to speak either from God or to him it becomes us to address ourselves to it with a solemn pause, and so to set bounds about the mount on which God is to come down, and not be hasty to utter any thing. It was in a still small voice that the message was delivered, and this was it (v. 17): "Shall mortal man be more just than God, the immortal God? Shall a man be thought to be, or pretend to be, more pure than his Maker? Away with such a thought!" 1. Some think that Eliphaz aims hereby to prove that Job's great afflictions were a certain evidence of his being a wicked man. A mortal man would be thought unjust and very impure if he should thus correct and punish a servant or subject, unless he had been guilty of some very great crime: "If therefore there were not some great crimes for which God thus punishes thee, man would be more just than God, which is not to be imagined." 2. I rather think it is only a reproof of Job's murmuring and discontent: "Shall a man pretend to be more just and pure than God? more truly to understand, and more strictly to observe, the rules and laws of equity than God? Shall Enosh, mortal and miserable man, be so insolent; nay, shall Geber, the strongest and most eminent man, man at his best estate, pretend to compare with God, or stand in competition with him?" Note, It is most impious and absurd to think either others or ourselves more just and pure than God. Those that quarrel and find fault with the directions of the divine law, the dispensations of the divine grace, or the disposals of the divine providence, make themselves more just and pure than God; and those who thus reprove God, let them answer it. What! sinful man! (for he would not have been mortal if he had not been sinful) short-sighted man! Shall he pretend to be more just, more pure, than God, who, being his Maker, is his Lord and owner? Shall the clay contend with the potter? What justice and purity there is in man, God is the author of it, and therefore is himself more just and pure. See Ps. 94:9, 10.

IV. The comment which Eliphaz makes upon this, for so it seems to be; yet some take all the following verses to be spoken in vision. It comes all to one.

1. He shows how little the angels themselves are in comparison with God, v. 18. Angels are God's servants, waiting servants, working servants; they are his ministers (Ps. 104:4); bright and blessed beings they are, but God neither needs them nor is benefited by them and is himself infinitely above them, and therefore, (a.) He puts no trust in them, did not repose a confidence in them, as we do in those we cannot live without. There is no service in which he employs them but, if he pleased, he could have it done as well without them. he never made them his confidants, or of his cabinet-council, Mt. 24:36. He does not leave his business wholly to them, but his own eyes run to and fro through the earth, 2 Chr. 16:9. See this phrase, ch. 39:11. Some give this sense of it: "So mutable is even the angelical nature that God would not trust angels with their own integrity; if he had, they would all have done as some did, left their

first estate; but he saw it necessary to give them supernatural grace to confirm them."

(b.) He charges them with folly, vanity, weakness, infirmity, and imperfection, in comparison with himself. If the world were left to the government of the angels, and they were trusted with the sole management of affairs, they would take false steps, and everything would not be done for the best, as now it is. Angels are intelligences, but finite ones. Though not chargeable with iniquity, yet with imprudence. This last clause is variously rendered by the critics. I think it would bear this reading, repeating the negation, which is very common: He will put no trust in his saints; nor will he glory in his angels (in angelis suis non ponet gloriationem) or make his boast of them, as if their praises, or services, added any thing to him: it is his glory that he is infinitely happy without them.

2. Thence he infers how much less man is, how much less to be trusted in or gloried in. If there is such a distance between God and angels, what is there between God and man!

See how man is represented here in his meanness. (1.) Look upon man in his life, and he is very mean, v. 19. Take man in his best estate, and he is a very despicable creature in comparison with the holy angels, though honourable if compared with the brutes. It is true, angels are spirits, and the souls of men are spirits; but, [1.] Angels are pure spirits; the souls of men dwell in houses of clay: such the bodies of men are. Angels are free; human souls are housed, and the body is a cloud, a clog, to it; it is its cage; it is its prison. It is a house of clay, mean and mouldering; an earthen vessel, soon broken, as it was first formed, according to the good pleasure of the potter. It is a cottage, not a house of cedar or a house of ivory, but of clay, which would soon be in ruins if not kept in constant repair. [2.] Angels are fixed, but the very foundation of that house of clay in which man dwells is in the dust. A house of clay, if built upon a rock, might stand long; but, if founded in the dust, the uncertainty of the foundation will hasten its fall, and it will sink with its own weight. As man was made out of the earth, so he is maintained and supported by that which cometh out of the earth. Take away that, and his body returns to its earth. We stand but upon the dust; some have a higher heap of dust to stand upon than others, but still it is the earth that stays us up and will shortly swallow us up. [3.] Angels are immortal, but man is soon crushed; the earthly house of his tabernacle is dissolved; he dies and wastes away, is crushed like a moth between one's fingers, as easily, as quickly; one may almost as soon kill a man as kill a moth. A little thing will destroy his life. He is crushed before the face of the moth, so the word is. If some lingering distemper, which consumes like a moth, be commissioned to destroy him, he can no more resist it than he can resist an acute distemper, which comes roaring upon him like a lion. See Hos. 5:12-14. Is such a creature as this to be trusted in, or can any service be expected from him by that God who puts no trust in angels themselves?

(2.) Look upon him in his death, and he appears yet more despicable, and unfit to be trusted. Men are mortal and dying, v. 20, 21. [1.] In death they are destroyed, and perish for ever, as to this world; it is the final period of their lives, and all the employments and enjoyments here; their place will know them no more. [2.] They are dying daily, and continually wasting: Destroyed from morning to evening. Death is still working in us, like a mole digging our grave at each remove, and we so continually lie exposed that we are killed all the day long. [3.] Their life is short, and in a little time they are cut off. It lasts perhaps but from morning to evening. It is but a day (so some understand it); their birth and death are but the sun-rise and sun-set of the same day. [4.] In death all their excellency passes away; beauty, strength, learning, not only cannot secure them from death, but must die with them, nor shall their pomp, their wealth, or power, descend after them. [5.] Their wisdom cannot save them from death: They die without wisdom, die for want of wisdom, by their own foolish management of themselves, digging their graves with their own teeth. [6.] It is so common a thing that nobody heeds it, nor takes any notice of it: They perish without any regarding it, or laying it to heart. The deaths of others are much the subject of common talk, but little the subject of serious thought. Some think the eternal damnation of sinners is here spoken of, as well as their temporal death: They are destroyed, or broken to pieces, by death, from morning to evening; and, if they repent not, they perish for ever (so some read it), v. 20. They perish for ever because they regard not God and their duty; they consider not their latter end, Lam. 1:9. They have no excellency but that which death takes away, and they die, they die the second death, for want of wisdom to lay hold on eternal life. Shall such a mean, weak, foolish, sinful, dying creature as this pretend to be more just than God and more pure than his Maker? No, instead of quarrelling with his afflictions, let him wonder that he is out of hell.

My challenge to you is to face the truth about where you are in your life today and choose how you will react to what is staring back at you in the mirror!

The Holy Spirit searches the hearts of mankind and can reveal areas that we have not seen.

Take authority over the past and declare and decree that their hold has been removed from your life. His sheep know his voice and a stranger he will not follow. Forgive those who have harmed you in any way and release the negativity. Release yourself from generation failings and use them as milestones and memorials that will prevent you from walking and embracing them as yours. Becauset the Bible says that no longer will the childrens teeth be set on edge!

Behold, the days come, saith the Lord, that I will sow the house of Israel and the house of Judah with the seed of man, and with the seed of beast. And it shall come to pass, that like as I have watched over them, to pluck up, and to break down, and to throw down, and to destroy, and to afflict; so will I watch over them, to build, and to plant, saith the Lord. In those days they shall say no more, The fathers have eaten a sour grape, and the children's teeth are set on edge. But every one shall die for his own iniquity: every man that eateth the sour grape, his teeth shall be set on edge. -- Jeremiah 31: 27-30 (KJV)

So any failures you may have experienced in the past that are connected to your past generations must be turned into teachable moments to train and shape your spirit according to the Word of the Living God! Ask the Holy Spirit to set a watch and guard over your speech especillay over your mouth. Because…

"The limit of my language is the limit of my world." -- Wittgenstein

Face your fears and not flee from them because you can only gain the victory over what you will confront! Get as much of an understanding as possible of the events and the circumstances surrounding the events and face it fully persuaded that God is able to empower you to overcome as in II Timothy 1: 7.

Surround yourself with relationships that are whole in the areas where you have been weakened until you are restored and rebuilt!

Study the Bible and restake your claim, build again, love again, try again and above all else stop the cycle of victimization and become the Victor and somebodys' Hero!

He who exercises no forethought but makes light of his opponents is sure to be captured by them.

The clever combatant imposes his will on the enemy but does not allow the enemy's will to be imposed on him. Do not repeat the tactics which have gained you one victory, but let your methods be regulated by the infinite variety of circumstances.

Tactics are like water; for water in its natural course runs away from high places and hastens downwards. Water shapes its course according to the nature of the ground over which it flows; we must work out strategy in relation to the foe we are facing.

Therefore, just as water retains no constant shape, so in battle there are no constant conditions.

He who can modify his tactics in relation to his opponent and thereby succeed in winning, may be called a heaven-born captain.

> Walking into a fight without a weapon fit for the battle you are in is suicidal! Ephesians 6, speaks of the whole armour of God; which are weapons of offense and defense. We are tossed to and fro with every wind and doctrine when we are immature, carnal and double-minded in battle times!

We must be deliberate and full of purpose and that is full of God's purpose and not our own.

Purpose

Purpose, meaning one who intends to accomplish or attain an intent, design, aim, end, object, objective, or goal. Intention – implies little more than what one has in mind to do or bring about. Intent – suggests clearer formulation or greater deliberateness. Design – implies a more carefully calculated plan and carefully ordered details and sometimes scheming. Aim – adds implications of effort clearly directed toward attaining or accomplishing. End – stresses the intended effect of action often in distinction or contrast to the action or means as such. Object – may equal end but more often applies to a more individually determined wish or need. Objective – implies something tangible and immediately attainable. Goal – suggests something attained only by prolonged effort and hardship.

Imagine seeing the enemy advance on you and you are not sure which choice to make, flee, fight or surrender!

God has not given us a spirit of fear he said, but of a sound mind! And that if we would think on the things that are lovely, pure and of good report that he would keep our minds in perfect peace.

I recall ministering to a Christian who told me they did not know what peace looked like or felt like! Because their whole life had been and was presently nothing but turmoil! Shocked, I began to share with them my experience with the peace of God and asked them to take a journey with me in our minds as I described a place of peace to them! They began to weep and sense the peace but could not embrace it! Whatever you have been through up to this point in your life has been detrimental to your emotional, physical, sexual and spiritual well being. You are possibly an unarmed man or inadequately armed for the battle that you are in or are about to face up ahead!

An Armed Man

The whole armour of God follows Ephesians 6:10, 11, 13-14 10 Finally, my brethren, be strong in the Lord, and in the power of his might. 11 Put on the whole armour of God, that ye may be able to stand against the wiles of the devil…13 Wherefore take unto you the whole armour of God, that ye may be able to withstand in the evil day, and having done all, to stand. 14 Stand therefore, having your loins girt about with truth,

Truthfulness:

In the Romans Soldiers arsenal the girdle was the key component to their ability to withstand against the adversaries they faced with full assurance they were protected. The girdle around their most sensitive and vulnerable place became the resting place for the rest of the armor. The centerpiece if you would upon which every other part was attached. The Bible says that it "Truth" in John 8:32 says that we must know the truth because it shall make us free, and in John 14:6-7 Jesus says, "…I am the way, the truth, and the life: no man cometh unto the Father, but by me. 7 If ye had known me, ye should have known my Father also: and from henceforth ye know him, and have seen him."

You SEE Jesus is THE TRUTH that our girdle represents, the whole armour of God rest on THE TRUTH "Jesus" In him we are known as we really are no deception, or shadows or turning.

A lie and a liar cannot stand up to A TRUTH from GOD THE TRUTH of GOD! Jesus is THE TRUTH, Jesus often tells us "A" Truth in the Bible, but clearly He says "I AM The TRUTH." He said to those around if that had believed that then they would know him and his father.

Breastplate of Righteousness

Guard your heart, because out of the heart flow the issues of life and death as in Proverbs 4:23 (KJV) Keep thy heart with all diligence; for out of it are the issues of life. We are the righteousness of God (the life of God) Zoe that was lost during the fall and restored to us at the obedience of God's son Jesus Christ! Again that piece of Armor points to Jesus and since we are the righteousness of God – THROUGH – Christ Jesus! When we say we are unable to live up to the standards of God's expectations for us we speak a lie, because we are being empowered by the Spirit of Truth to do and be as one who is seated on the right hand of God.

Feet Shod

Shoes on in the preparation of the gospel of peace;..." the shoes worn during times of war by the Roman soldiers were called caligas and securely fitted like an athlete laces his shoes for game time around their ankles, and the soles were impregnated with nails that gave the stability of hinds feet of a deer for balancing up the inclines and valleys allowing them to keep pace without their feet getting caught. Can you imagine fighting for your life and being unable to keep your footing Brings you peace knowing that your steps are sure; meaning you are confident in the direction you are headed and your ability to stand in the battle gives solace for those who are following you and whom you are following. Because they know your steps are ordered of the Lord and your mind is full of The Truth and your Heart is kept on and by The Truth, therefore you will not follow a lie or give faulty directions

Shield of Faith

wherewith ye shall be able to quench all the fiery darts of the wicked..." It is custom made for you just like the other pieces of your armor. Your height and width was taken into consideration when this piece of armor was made to allow you to be fully covered as you faced the enemy. It was soaked in water to extinguish the flaming arrows that were being shot at you the moment it touched your shield. No matter what comes at you as long as you are fully persuaded that God is for you!

Helmet of Salvation

to cover that head! I am reminded of an old church song, that said something like this. What do you know about Jesus, and the chorus He's Alright! Tell me what you know about Jesus, and the chorus He's Alright! Your mind must be persuaded and your heart fixed that you know Him and that He's Alright! They would say, well I tried him as a doctor, and the chorus would say; He's Alright, and on and on they would come up with inexhaustible ways they had tried him for themselves. They had learned to magnify God in their minds, well the helmet of salvation is like that; because affixed to the helmets top were a tall grouping of feathers that stood above the shield and the enemy had difficulty gauging exactly how tall you really were. Proverb says, "As a Man Thinketh, So Is He." If you think you are defeated, then you are. A soldier must not allow themselves to be on the battlefield wavering (detouring) from THE TRUTH! You must KNOW THE TRUTH, and that is JESUS CHRIST!

Sword of the Spirit

which is how you come to know that he is ALRIGHT! Through studying the word of God in

II Timothy 2:15, "15 Study to shew thyself approved unto God, a workman that needeth not to be ashamed, rightly dividing the word of truth." The Word of God inside of you makes you stand tall internally, so that it is projected onto the outer man and when you are fully clothed in the Armour of God you my dear friend have done nothing less than put on your robe of righteousness which is through Christ Jesus and which is none other than the Lord Jesus Christ himself!

Romans 13:14 But put ye on the Lord Jesus Christ, and make not provision for the flesh, to fulfil the lusts thereof.

The Colicky Lust of the Flesh

Flesh is like a screaming, colicky baby that has ingested air and has a distended belly and can not get any relief. Everything in the house is on edge because the child can not be appeased easily! Unbridled desires and pursuits are like a colicky baby, difficult to appease.

How do you spell relief when your flesh is colicky!

Do you look for it in people, objects or thrills What would you do if you had just been denied satisfaction Would you be consolable or out of control How does God intend for you to reel in your flesh when you are so deeply in times where your needs scream unreasonably for relief. The best way for me to describe this feeling – is when you know food is available and you have not made up your mind what you want to eat, but you have been thinking about eating all day and you did not eat breakfast or lunch, and now it is dinner time and the first thing you can get your hands on is what you eat, but you are not really satisfied. So, you snack and munch and eat the rest of the night. Mindful that the portion of the food you ate should have satisfied you based on the serving size. But it is something about eating what you have a desire for that does not leave you with a need for something else to satisfy you. You eat it and immediately you know to yourself that is what I have been wanting all day long! Sin to me is like that, you want sex, but you want it a certain way and with a certain person! You want to shop but you want to shop in a certain mall or store, for a certain item; you find bargains along the way that should make you stop looking for that item. But you are not satisfied because you did not obtain what your desire was set on! You have gone from your thought life to your eye gate and engaged every one of your senses in seeking satisfaction only to discover that it is temporary gratification. It takes more of the same thing to get the same feeling! You never get to feel that fleeting feeling again quite the same way! Now our eyes are full of darkness! And if your eye be full of darkness then so is your whole body!

The Lust of the Eyes

Self-denial blinds and darkens the window of the eye of the soul. The eyes are said to be the window to the soul. When the eyes are dark the view is affected inward and outwardly. Being full of darkness pretending to be enlightened, but these are the light is dim. There are spirits that manifest in the pupil of the eyes when the body is full of darkness or shadows of turning are present. My experience with the visibility of these spirits is worth noting because they are deceptive. When a person whose under the influence of the spirits walk by and looked back as a glance their eyes literally have an orbital range that appears as if their eyes are looking backward. Your eyes lock on theirs and your breath is captivated and adrenalin races and what you see must be oppressed or possessed of the enemy. A person tormented by a lascivious spirit appearance in their eyes can sometimes be similar to a ravenous animal. Lasciviousness has entered in and caused them to have uncontrollable urges makes them predatory! The hunt for prey is on and the hunt for what will satisfy this voracious appetite! This spirit devours without getting satisfaction; and must increase the quest for fulfillment. It becomes obsessed with self and roams to and fro like Satan looking for whom they may devour!

The lust of the eyes looks at the things which are seen and become stimulated to the point of obsession over an outwardly attractive person, and once we take the wrapper off and play with it a little while; the beast appears and then it is too late to withdraw! There are beautiful people who are beautiful through and through and there is nothing wrong with that! But when your number one criteria is to seek after the flesh of that person and not their spirit, you are asking for a double dose of misery.

Satan perverts and blinds us with the secret desires of our hearts. When a woman's husband leaves for another woman less attractive or less sophisticated and accomplished than she is. She becomes highly offended, her pride is wounded and more than anything it creates a large void deep within her that makes her question her own beauty; and thus she becomes subconsciously insecure.

Creating an opening for one to become obsessed with the worlds way of doing and being. After all the world infers that beauty is not fleeting or fading with all the means presented to keep a youthful appearance. The spirt of God moved, brooded over the face of the deep that was without form or void and drew from within that void to himself and drew out the beauty that was concealed or hidden in what seemed useless. The pride of life will cause you to look to the world for remedies and potions and procedures to maintain, or attempt to hold onto what has been diminished through inappropriate usage. Excessiveness and gluttony of life as in Luke 7:34 and Proverbs 23:20

This scorned woman wonders and exclaims to anyone who will listen, 'what does he see in her

What she has failed to realize the less attractive woman may have spent more time seeking the face of God and allowing him to display her inner beauty, and thus on display is a certain confidence outwardly that makes her a more attractive counterpart. What is on the inside of a person will show up on the outside, sooner or later.

David said in Psalms 37:31 that this man, who has the law of his God in his heart; will see none of his steps slide. I believe we can even believe that God would be our greatest potion and remedy along with proper care of ourselves not allow us to slide in our faces or extremities. After all he is the manufacturer!

Jeremiah said in Chapter 32:39, "…that those who do these things will be his people, and he their God, and I will give them one heart, and one way, that they may fear me forever, for the good of them, and of their children after them…I will put my fear in their hearts, that they shall not depart from me...yea, I will rejoice over them to do them good, and I will plant them in this land assuredly with my whole heart and with my whole soul." We have a form of godliness that denies the power thereof. The word in Hebrew 'Dabaq' means to cleave, to be attached, devoted, and to hang upon.

One who dabaqs' God can be built upon as a church that the gates of hell can not prevail against!

If we will be willing and obedient we will eat the good of the land! Then the Lord shall command the blessing upon thee in thy storehouses, and in all that thou settest thine hand unto; and he shall bless thee in the land which the Lord thy God giveth thee…if that thou hearken unto the commandments of the Lord thy God, which I command thee this day, to observe and to do them: And thou shalt not go aside from any of the words which I command thee this day, to the right hand, or to the left, to go after other gods to serve them."

Remember the patterned life of one who accepts, receives, and applies the divine order for his life is the righteous man who follows these steps:

"BLESSED IS the man that walketh not in the counsel of the ungodly, nor standeth in the way of sinners, nor sitteth in the seat of the scornful. But his delight is in the law of the Lord; and in his law doth he meditate day and night. And he shall be like a tree planted by the rivers of water, that bringeth forth his fruit in his season; his leaf also shall not wither; and whatsoever he doeth shall prosper…

BUT …

the ungodly are not so: but are like the chaff which the wind driveth away. Therefore the ungodly shall not stand in the judgment, nor sinners in the congregation of the righteous.

For the Lord knoweth the way of the righteous; but the way of the ungodly shall perish."

A blessed man is an obedient man. That man is like a tree planted by the rivers of water. That man is not a sinner (oops) but a righteous man. One who practices the way of God and walks therein. The whole conclusion of God's purpose for our lives!

Everything else is the outworking of the inworking of Deuteronomy 28 and Psalms 1. Your calling and election are manifestations of your inward walk of righteousness, and the method by which God chooses to express your inward walk.

Such as Apostle, Prophet, Teacher, Evangelist, or Pastor.

The ability to operate with ease in these comes from the fruit of the spirit, which is the outward flow of your love walk.

The love of God is shed abroad from breast to breast! The gifts of the spirit operate like a gauge on a car measuring the amount of gas in your car. The effectiveness of your gifts are a direct relationship to the measure of anointing in your life. In Deuteronomy 6:5 "Love the Lord your God with all your heart, and all your soul, and with all your strength." Instead we seek to gain our life, and ultimately we lose it!

Let's look at Psalms 59:

1.
To the chief Musician, Altaschith, Michtam of David; when Saul sent, and they watched the house to kill him. Deliver me from mine enemies, O my God: defend me from them that rise up against me.
2.
 Deliver me from the workers of iniquity, and save me from bloody men.
3.
For, lo, they lie in wait for my soul: the mighty are gathered against me; not for my transgression, nor for my sin, O LORD.
4.
They run and prepare themselves without my fault: awake to help me, and behold.
5.
Thou therefore, O LORD God of hosts, the God of Israel, awake to visit all the heathen: be not merciful to any wicked transgressors. Selah.
6.
They return at evening: they make a noise like a dog, and go round about the city.
7.
Behold, they belch out with their mouth: swords are in their lips: for who, say they, doth hear?

8.
But thou, O LORD, shalt laugh at them; thou shalt have all the heathen in derision.
9.
Because of his strength will I wait upon thee: for God is my defence.
10.
The God of my mercy shall prevent me: God shall let me see my desire upon mine enemies.
11.
Slay them not, lest my people forget: scatter them by thy power; and bring them down, O Lord our shield.
12.
For the sin of their mouth and the words of their lips let them even be taken in their pride: and for cursing and lying which they speak.
13.
Consume them in wrath, consume them that they may not be: and let them know that God ruleth in Jacob unto the ends of the earth. Selah.
14.
And at evening let them return; and let them make a noise like a dog, and go round about the city.
15.
Let them wander up and down for meat, and grudge if they be not satisfied. Each evening they come back, howling like dogs and prowling about the city. They roam about for food and growl if they do not get their fill.

16.
But I will sing of thy power; yea, I will sing aloud of thy mercy in the morning: for thou hast been my defence and refuge in the day of my trouble.
17.
Unto thee, O my strength, will I sing: for God is my defence, and the God of my mercy.

And also at Psalm 42

1 through 3

A white-tailed deer drinks from the creek; I want to drink God, deep draughts of God. I'm thirsty for God-alive. I wonder, "Will I ever make it — arrive and drink in God's presence?" I'm on a diet of tears— tears for breakfast, tears for supper. All day long people knock at my door, pestering, "Where is this God of yours?"
4
These are the things I go over and over, emptying out the pockets of my life. I was always at the head of the worshiping crowd, right out in front, Leading them all, eager to arrive and worship, Shouting praises, singing thanksgiving— celebrating, all of us, God's feast!
5
Why are you down in the dumps, dear soul? Why are you crying the blues? Fix my eyes on God— soon I'll be praising again. He puts a smile on my face. He's my God.

6-8
When my soul is in the dumps, I rehearse everything I know of you, From Jordan depths to Hermon heights, including Mount Mizar. Chaos calls to chaos, to the tune of whitewater rapids. Your breaking surf, your thundering breakers crash and crush me. Then God promises to love me all day, sing songs all through the night! My life is God's prayer.

9-10
Sometimes I ask God, my rock-solid God, "Why did you let me down? Why am I walking around in tears, harassed by enemies?" They're out for the kill, these tormentors with their obscenities, Taunting day after day, "Where is this God of yours?"

11
Why are you down in the dumps, dear soul? Why are you crying the blues? Fix my eyes on God— soon I'll be praising again. He puts a smile on my face. He's my God.

The place of sanctuary is found when we as believers run into the shelter of the Most High by creating a presence of thanksgiving and praise, faith and love and the application of the blood of Jesus to our dwelling places. Be they our physical and/or spiritual houses. We see Habakkuk in chapter 3:17-19, making a declaration of the faithfulness of our sovereign God! 17 Though the fig tree does not bud and there are no grapes on the vines, though the olive crop fails and the fields produce no food, though there are no sheep in the pen and no cattle in the stalls, 18 yet I will rejoice in the LORD, I will be joyful in God my Savior. 19 The Sovereign LORD is my strength; he makes my feet like the feet of a deer, he enables me to go on the heights.

God placed inside of each of his human creations the need to have the following seven godly things to be fulfilled!

Dignity

1. God Created Us with a Need for Dignity "Then God said, 'Let us make man in our image, in our likeness,' ...So God created man in his own image, in the image of God he created him; male and female he created them" Gen. 1:26,27).

Authority

2. God Created Us with a Need for Authority "And let them rule over the fish of the sea and the birds of the air, over the livestock, over all the earth, and over all the creatures that move along the ground" (Gen. 1:26).

Blessing and Provision

3. God Created Us with a Need for Blessing and Provision "God blessed them and said to them, 'Be fruitful and increase in number; fill the earth and subdue it. Rule over the fish of the sea and the birds of the air and over every living creature that moves on the ground.' Then God said, 'I give you every seed-bearing plant on the face of the whole earth and every tree that has fruit with seed in it. They will be yours for food'" (Gen. 1:28,29).

Security

4. God Created Us with a Need for Security "Now the Lord God had planted a garden in the east, in Eden; and there he put the man he had formed. And the Lord God made all kinds of trees grow out of the ground —

trees that were pleasing to the eye and good for food. In the middle of the garden were the tree of life and the tree of the knowledge of good and evil" (Gen. 2:8,9).

Purpose and Meaning

5. God Created Us with a Need for Purpose and Meaning.

"The Lord God took the man and put him in the Garden of Eden to work it and take care of it. ...Now the Lord God had formed out of the ground all the beasts of the field and all the birds of the air. He brought them to the man to see what he would name them; and whatever the man called each living creature, that was its name" (Gen. 2:15,19).

Freedom and Boundary

6. God Created Us with a Need for Freedom and Boundary

"And the Lord God commanded the man, 'You are free to eat from any tree in the garden; but you must not eat from the tree of the knowledge of good and evil, for when you eat of it you will surely die'" (Gen. 2:16,17).

Intimate Love and Companionship

7. God Created Us to Experience Intimate Love and Companionship:

"The Lord God said, 'It is not good for the man to be alone. I will make a helper suitable for him'" (Genesis 2:18). "For Adam no suitable helper was found. So the Lord God caused the man to fall into a deep sleep; and while he was sleeping, he took one of the man's ribs and closed up the place with flesh. Then the Lord God made a woman from the rib he had taken out of the man, and he brought her to the man. The man said, 'This is now bone of my bones and flesh of my flesh; she shall be called "woman", for she was taken out of man.' For this reason a man will leave his father and mother and be united to his wife, and they will become one flesh. The man and his wife were both naked, and they felt no shame" (Gen. 2:20-25).

Remember, after the strongholds are demolished, you still have the responsibility to take your thoughts captive. Paraphrasing Paul, "You can't listen to the demonic voices and hear the voice of Jesus too."

Pray Now:

Father in heaven, I recognize the power You have given me by the shed blood of Jesus to demolish strongholds in my life. I confess that I have given a foothold to the sin(s) of _____.
I renounce the stronghold of _____ by the authority of the Name of Jesus Christ according to Your Word. I take back through Your power that ground that I surrendered to the enemy and pray that You will fill me with trust-grounded obedience to Your Holy Spirit so that this area of my life will be in conformity to the image of Christ. In Jesus' Name I pray. Amen.

Endnotes

MATERIALS
Bibles: King James Version

Books:
Myles Munroe, copyright 1991
Single, Married, Separated & Life After Divorce
Bahamas Faith Ministries Published by Vincom, Inc.
P.O. Box 702400
Tulsa, OK 74170
Reprint Permission Granted by Vincom, Inc.

Eugenia Price
Woman to Woman, copyright 1959
Zondervan Books
Zondervan Publishing House
Grand Rapids, MI 49506
Used by Permission of Zondervan Publishing House

Derek and Ruth Prince
God Is A Matchmaker, 1986
Chosen Books a Division of Baker Book House
P.O. Box 6287
Grand Rapids, MI 49516-6287
Used by Permission of Baker Book House

Spiros Zodhiates
The Complete Word Study – New Testament
Chattanooga, TN 37422
AMG Publishers, 1991
6815 Shallowford Rd.
Box 22000
Reprint Permission Granted by AMG Publishers

Volumes in the One Heart Series

VOLUME 1
With Oneness of Heart
ISBN 0-9700976-0-3
Formats: Paper, Audio, E-Book & Digital, Kindle

VOLUME 2
Book: Journeying to the Road Called Oneness
ISBN 0-9700976-1-1
Formats: Paper, Audio, E-Book & Digital, Kindle

VOLUME 3
Detouring off the Road of Oneness
ISBN 0-9700976-2-X
Formats: Paper, Audio, E-Book & Digital, Kindle
Book: Disciple's Guide
Audio: Disciple's Overview

VOLUME 4
I and My Father Are One
ISBN 0-9700976-3-8
Formats: Paper, Audio, E-Book & Digital, Kindle
 Book: Disciple's Guide
Audio: Disciple's Overview

VOLUME 5
52 Week Devotional & Journal Study/Application
ISBN 09700976-7-0
Formats: Paperback

Other Books by Patricia E. Adams cont'd

Set Free to Praise Him: A Childs' Rights Violated
"Her Terrors and Traumas"
ISBN 0-9700976-5-4

Salvation "Soteria" More Than a Ticket to Heaven,
 ISBN 0-9700976-4-6

Shortcuts Consequences
ISBN 0-9700976-6-2

Help My Fears Shadow is Chasing Me
ISBN 0-9700976-8-9

Fiery Darts of the Assassin
ISBN 0-9700976-9-7

www.ingramcontent.com/pod-product-compliance
Lightning Source LLC
Chambersburg PA
CBHW050557170426
43201CB00011B/1729